The Complete Guide to German Shorthaired Pointers

Dr. Joanna de Klerk

LP Media Inc. Publishing

Text copyright © 2020 by LP Media Inc.

All rights reserved.

No part of this book may be reproduced or transmitted in any form or by any means, electronic or mechanical, including photocopying, recording, or by an information storage and retrieval system - except by a reviewer who may quote brief passages in a review to be printed in a magazine or newspaper - without permission in writing from the publisher. For information address LP Media Inc. Publishing, 3178 253rd Ave. NW, Isanti, MN 55040

www.lpmedia.org

Publication Data

Dr. Joanna de Klerk

The Complete Guide to German Shorthaired Pointers---- First edition.

Summary: "Successfully raising a German Shorthaired Pointer from puppy to old age" --- Provided by publisher.

ISBN: 978-1-952069-70-3

[1.German Shorthaired Pointers --- Non-Fiction] I. Title.

This book has been written with the published intent to provide accurate and authoritative information in regard to the subject matter included. While every reasonable precaution has been taken in preparation of this book the author and publisher expressly disclaim responsibility for any errors, omissions, or adverse effects arising from the use or application of the information contained inside. The techniques and suggestions are to be used at the reader's discretion and are not to be considered a substitute for professional veterinary care. If you suspect a medical problem with your dog, consult your veterinarian.

Design by Sorin Rădulescu

First paperback edition, 2020

Cover Photo Courtesy of Jenna Stankiewicz

TABLE OF CONTENTS

ACKNOWLEDGMENTS ... 9

CHAPTER 1
Breed History ... 10
Origin of the Breed ... 10
The Rise of the German Empire Middle-Class ... 11
The Challenges of German Hunting ... 12
Breed Ancestry ... 13
Famous German Shorthaired Pointers ... 16

CHAPTER 2
About the Breed ... 18
Appearance ... 19
Official Standard for the German Shorthaired Pointer (AKC 1992) ... 20
Age Expectancy ... 25
Inside the Home ... 26
Outside the Home ... 27

CHAPTER 3
Behavior ... 30
Temperament and Personality ... 30
Importance of Socialization ... 33
Exercise Requirements ... 35
Common Behavior Problems ... 37

CHAPTER 4
How to Choose a German Shorthaired Pointer ... 40
Purchasing or Rescuing? ... 40
Male or Female? ... 45
Researching the Establishment ... 46
Inquire About the Parents and Health Tests ... 49
Looking at the Puppy ... 51
Considerations of a Rescue Dog ... 53
Reasons for Not Choosing a German Shorthaired Pointer ... 55

CHAPTER 5
Preparations for a New Dog ... 56
Preparing the Outside of Your House ... 57
Preparing the Inside of Your House ... 60
Shopping List ... 64
Crates ... 64
Beds ... 66
Collars, Harnesses and Leashes ... 67
Bowls ... 68
Toys and Accessories ... 69
Introducing Your New German Shorthaired Pointer to Other Dogs ... 70
Preparing Children to Meet Your New GSP ... 72

CHAPTER 6
Basic Training ... 74
Treat, Toy or Clicker? ... 75
Potty Training ... 79
Obedience Training ... 81
How to Teach Sit ... 82
How to Teach Lie Down ... 83
How to Teach Stay ... 83
How to Teach Walk on the Leash ... 85
How to Teach Walk Off the Leash ... 87
How to Teach Your German Shorthaired Pointer to be Left on His Own ... 88

CHAPTER 7
Introduction to Training for Field Work ... 90
Types of Hunting ... 91
Choosing a Hunting Puppy ... 92
Expanding on Basic Training ... 95
The E-Collar Debate ... 96
Teaching Discipline ... 99
Teaching Retrieving ... 100
Introduction to the Gun ... 101
Introduction to Water ... 103
Training in the Field ... 103
Ethical Handling of Gundogs ... 106
Field Trials and Tests ... 106

CHAPTER 8
Nutrition ... 110

Importance of Nutrition **110**
Commercial Food **111**
Pet Food Labels **112**
BARF and Homemade Diets **115**
Weight Monitoring **116**

CHAPTER 9
Traveling **118**
Preparations for Travel **119**
Traveling in a Car **121**
Traveling by Plane **122**
Vacation Lodging **125**
Leaving Your German Shorthaired Pointer at Home **125**

CHAPTER 10
Dental Care **128**
Importance of Dental Care **129**
Dental Anatomy **129**
Tartar Build-Up and Gingivitis **130**
Dental Care **130**
Dental Procedures **132**

CHAPTER 11
Grooming **134**
About the Coat **135**
Coat Health **135**
Nail Clipping **137**
Ear Cleaning **138**
Anal Glands **139**

CHAPTER 12
Preventative Health Care **140**
Choosing a Veterinarian **141**
    Qualifications **141**
    After-Hours Emergencies **141**
    Extras **142**
Vaccinations **143**
Microchipping **144**
External Parasites **144**
Internal Parasites **146**
Neutering **146**
Pet Insurance **148**

CHAPTER 13
Breed-Specific Diseases — 150
- Diseases to Test For — 150
  - Progressive Retinal Atrophy — 151
  - Joint Dysplasia — 152
  - Aortic Stenosis — 153
  - Cone Degeneration (Day Blindness) — 153
  - Von Willebrand's Disease — 153
  - Skin Diseases — 154
  - Lupus Erythematosus — 155
  - Yeast Dermatitis — 155
  - Acral Mutilation Syndrome — 156
- Digestive Diseases — 156
  - Gastric Dilation Volvulus — 156
  - Hepatitis — 157
  - Myasthenia Gravis — 157
- Mobility Diseases — 157
  - Cruciate Ligament Disease — 159
  - Panosteitis — 159

CHAPTER 14
Adult Life — 160
- Pet Life — 161
  - Running Partner — 162
  - Hiking Partner — 164
  - Fun Sport – Agility and Flyball — 165
- Guard Dog Life — 167
- Show Life — 169
- Stud Life — 171

CHAPTER 15
Living with a Senior Dog — 174
- Diet — 175
- Senior Wellness Checks — 177
- Advanced Arthritis — 177
- Mental Deterioration — 179
- Organ Deterioration — 180
- Loss of Senses — 181
- Bladder Control — 182
- Lifestyle Modifications — 184
- Saying Goodbye — 184

ACKNOWLEDGMENTS

I would like to thank everyone who has contributed information to enable me to compile this book. Through my work as a vet in clinical practice and complementary medicine, I've come to realize that German Shorthaired Pointers are completely unique dogs, which require a specific type of training and care. It has been incredibly interesting developing my knowledge of the breed during my research for this book, and I have a new-found respect for German Shorthaired Pointer owners!

I would also like to thank my editor, Clare Hardy, who plays an instrumental role in all my writing work. I am so grateful for her contribution and general dog knowledge and appreciate all her time helping me write some work I'm proud to put out there!

CHAPTER 1
Breed History

Origin of the Breed

There are two clues to the origins of the German Shorthaired Pointer in its name. The breed originated in Germany. And its purpose as a hunting dog is evident in the name Pointer.

A Pointer is a type of hunting dog used to locate game, after which they then freeze in the pointing position, allowing the hunter to move in on the quarry. The characteristic pointing posture is assumed when the dog freezes with its head lowered, keeping a steady gaze, and raising a front paw in a line like an arrow towards the prey. Before guns were used for hunting, the Pointer would locate a game bird in the wild, freeze to avoid flushing the bird before the huntsman was within range, and point to its location, allowing the huntsman to cast a net over the bird.

Pointers date all the way back to the Roman Empire, but the German Shorthaired Pointer (GSP) is believed to have emerged at the beginning of the 1800s, when it became distinct from its European ancestors due to being bred for the specific requirements of German huntsmen.

Photo Courtesy of Mariana Gonzalez

The name Pointer is slightly misleading in the case of the GSP. This is because although the breed is predominantly descended from Pointer bloodlines, and one of its major strengths is indeed in pointing for the huntsman, today's German Shorthaired Pointer is a multi-purpose hunting dog. This versatility was foremost in the objectives of the nineteenth-century breeders that developed and refined the dog we know today.

CHAPTER 1 Breed History

Photo Courtesy of Katie Holbrooks

The Rise of the German Empire Middle-Class

Hunting is a centuries-old tradition in Germany, but until the mid-1800s, it was the preserve of royalty and the aristocracy, simply because they owned the land and reserved the right to hunt on it.

During the mid-nineteenth century, economic and political changes in Europe led to a rise in the status and wealth of the middle class. With this came land ownership and hunting rights, so a growing proportion of the German population had the opportunity to hunt regularly. This gave impetus to the development of a breed of hunting dog specifically designed for the German terrain and methods of hunting.

The Challenges of German Hunting

During the nineteenth century, Germany was densely forested. This meant hunting on horseback, like the British, was not practical, and it was necessary for people to hunt on foot. The German hunting dog required a keen sense of smell to locate game from a good distance, when dense forest meant visibility was limited. The dog also needed to be disciplined to stay focused on its task and handler, and to remain on point once it had located the prey.

Apart from pointing, the German hunting dog needed a full range of hunting skills, including retrieving, both from land and water. And with a wide variety of animals calling the forests their home, such as deer, wild cats and foxes, the dog also needed to be bold enough to take on any animal it should encounter.

On top of that, German huntsmen wanted their dog to be capable of living in the family home as a guard dog and companion. Quite a tall order for any dog to meet such a wide variety of requirements, which is why the breed was successively refined over many decades, fine-tuned by careful introduction of many hunting breeds into the mix that we know as the German Shorthaired Pointer.

Photo Courtesy of Stephanie Clausel

CHAPTER 1   Breed History

Breed Ancestry

The earliest origins of the German Shorthaired Pointer are not known, as records were not kept until the breed first made the stud book in the 1870s. However, the common ancestor of all modern Pointer breeds is believed to be the Old Spanish Pointer, a breed that is now extinct, but which closely resembled today's Pachon Navarro.

Spanish dogs, trained by monks for hunting birds, were documented as far back as the first century. And when Muslim conquerors arrived on the Iberian Peninsula with their technique of falconry, they found that the Spanish dogs had a useful skill of pointing to locate their prey. Throughout the ensuing centuries, different European nations developed the Spanish Pointer into Pointers of their own. For example, the British favored speed and endurance for horseback hunting, so they crossed the Pointer with foxhound breeds, and the Germans were looking for scenting prowess and stealth, so they introduced bloodhounds and the French Gascon into the mix. This improved the trailing ability of the emerging German Pointer, and enhanced the dogs' boldness to enter the water, along with its aggression toward predators.

This early German Pointer had many qualities suited to the demands of his environment; however, he still had some shortcomings. For example, German huntsmen felt that the dog was not sufficiently fast or agile, and while they valued the scenting ability of the bloodhound, they wanted their dog to be sleeker in appearance. So, the fast and elegant English Pointer was brought in to refine the breed further. This fine-tuning resulted in

> **FUN FACT**
> **German Shorthaired Pointer Club of America (GSPCA)**
>
> The German Shorthaired Pointer Club of America (GSPCA) is the official American Kennel Club Parent Club for the GSP breed and was founded in 1938 in Minnesota. The first breed standard was approved in 1946, with subsequent revisions in 1976 and 1992. Membership in the club includes a copy of the official magazine, the Shorthair Journal, and access to seminars, Meet the Breed events, and other resources. More information can be found at the GSPCA website: www.gspca.org The German Shorthaired Pointer Club of America (GSPCA) is the official American Kennel Club Parent Club for the GSP breed and was founded in 1938 in Minnesota. The first breed standard was approved in 1946, with subsequent revisions in 1976 and 1992. Membership in the club includes a copy of the official magazine, the Shorthair Journal, and access to seminars, Meet the Breed events, and other resources. More information can be found at the GSPCA website: www.gspca.org

an impressively versatile breed, with beauty, brains and bravery, strength, stamina and an acute sense of smell. The dog was a loyal companion capable of taking on any game in the German field and forest.

By 1872, the German Shorthaired Pointer was ready for admission into the German Kennel Club Stud Book, with the appearance of the first breed ambassador, Hektor 1 ZK1. Not long afterwards, two competitors in the German Derby of 1883, Nero and Treff, became the foundation dogs for the breed.

The GSP rapidly became adopted across Europe and was taken to the US in 1925, where Nero's daughter Flora produced Walden, Waldo and Her-

Photo Courtesy of Jeff Marchant

CHAPTER 1   Breed History

Photo Courtesy of Andrew Cannata

tha, the progenitors of many of the pedigree lines in America. The American Kennel Club recognized the German Shorthaired Pointer in 1930, and in 2018, the GSP made the top ten of America's favorite breeds.

Ironically, just as the breed was rising to greater prominence outside Germany, the German breeding program was halted by World War II, with the best dogs sent to Yugoslavia to protect them. With the division of Germany after the war, West German breeders did not have access to the dogs in Eastern Europe, so the breed had to be started again, from a limited gene pool.

The GSP did not become popular in the UK until more recent times, since British huntsmen preferred their own breed of Pointer. But after World War II, the affectionate German Shorthaired Pointer found its way into the heart of the British nation, where it is now widely known and loved.

In 1962, two German Shorthaired Pointers named Dunpender Eva and Heathman of Friuli were taken from the UK to Australia, where they founded the Australian GSP dynasty. The breed was quickly recognized for its outstanding hunting capabilities and commanding presence in the show ring.

Famous German Shorthaired Pointers

As a busy working dog, the German Shorthaired Pointer doesn't have a lot of time for a celebrity life. However, there are a few GSPs worthy of an honorable mention in the Hall of Fame.

In literature, one of the first GSPs to appear was a dog named Bashan, who was immortalized in German author Thomas Mann's account of the bond with his dog in 1919. Bashan and I remains a classic. The New York Times stated that it is "the finest study of the mind of a dog ever written."

Another moving literary tribute to the German Shorthaired Pointer is found in Montana author Rick Bass's memoir, Colter: The True Story of the Best Dog I Ever Had (2001).

In fiction, author Robert B. Parker drew on his personal experience of the GSP in creating three successive companions to his main character, Bos-

Photo Courtesy of Chris and Lacy Kuhn

CHAPTER 1   Breed History

Photo Courtesy of Claude Doucette

ton detective Spenser. All three of Spenser's German Shorthairs were named Pearl. All were solid liver in color, but each had their own personalities.

In film, Terrence Mallick's 1978 classic Days of Heaven featured a brief appearance from national field champion Jocko von Stolzhafen. In the movie, Jocko is seen hunting in the prairie. Sadly, he disappeared without a trace a short while later, and was presumed to have been stolen.

Famous for his important role in twenty-first-century life, Haus is a GSP trained to use his remarkable scenting skills to sniff out explosives for the US Air Force. Also representing the breed is Pina, who sniffs boxes and crates for New York's and New Jersey's Transportation Security Administration.

CHAPTER 2
About the Breed

Although the German Shorthaired Pointer has risen rapidly in popularity in recent years, it is still a misunderstood breed. To some extent, the stunning good looks of the breed can be a disadvantage, as many people want to own such a beautiful dog, without realizing that the German Shorthaired Pointer needs a home that is committed to exercising his body and mind, and understanding all the natural instincts in his genetic mix.

So, what is the perfect home for a German Shorthaired Pointer? It is important to understand that the breed is energetic, and therefore, people who lead active outdoor lives will be ideal partners for the GSP. Although a working home is ideal, the GSP can also thrive as a family dog, but he needs lots of mental stimulation, so his owners need to be prepared to invest time in him. This includes taking him out into the countryside for plenty of exercise and space, as well as consistently training to keep the dog's active mind focused.

The German Shorthaired Pointer is very sociable and loves his people, but is rather boisterous around young children, so is better suited to an older family. He also hates to be left alone, so will need human company for much of the day. German Shorthaired Pointers are highly trainable, but slow to mature. All of these factors make them poorly suited to first-time dog owners. However, in the right hands, the GSP will make a wonderfully obedient, lovable and loyal companion.

Photo Courtesy of Shannon and Ryan Hughes

Appearance

Chapter 1 discussed the development of the German Shorthaired Pointer, and how various breeds were introduced into the mix to refine the GSP's performance and appearance. Naturally, as a hunting dog, the German Shorthaired Pointer is athletic, with every muscle defined beneath his smooth, glossy, short coat. He is also in perfect proportion, with a noble look and an alertness that proclaims his intelligence, while his friendly nature is evident in his gentle appearance and trusting eyes.

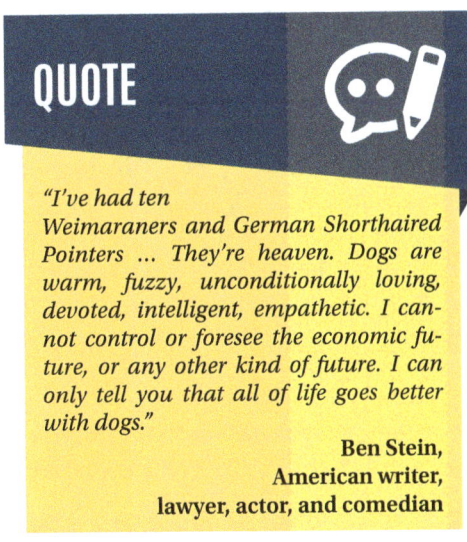

QUOTE

"I've had ten Weimaraners and German Shorthaired Pointers ... They're heaven. Dogs are warm, fuzzy, unconditionally loving, devoted, intelligent, empathetic. I cannot control or foresee the economic future, or any other kind of future. I can only tell you that all of life goes better with dogs."

Ben Stein, American writer, lawyer, actor, and comedian

The German Shorthaired Pointer may be found in a variety of color variations. The accepted breed colors are black, white and liver, and the breed can have spotted or ticked markings. The approved coat colors are:

- Black & White
- Black & White Spotted
- Black & White Spotted & Ticked
- Black & White Ticked
- Liver & White
- Liver & White Spotted
- Liver & White Spotted & Ticked
- Liver & White Ticked
- Liver Ticked
- Solid Black
- Solid Liver

As with any pedigree dog, the German Shorthaired Pointer should conform as closely as possible to the breed standard. Each country will have its own breed standard, and there may be slight variations, so if you plan to show your dog, it is important that you study the breed standard in your own country. However, even if you have no plans for showing, the breed standard is still important, as it is set out to ensure that the health and integrity of the breed is foremost in a breeder's mind. For this reason, the AKC Breed Standard is reproduced in full here as a useful reference:

Official Standard for the German Shorthaired Pointer (AKC 1992)

General Appearance: The German Shorthaired Pointer is a versatile hunter, an all-purpose gun dog capable of high performance in field and water. The judgment of Shorthairs in the show ring reflects this basic characteristic. The overall picture which is created in the observer's eye is that of an aristocratic, well balanced, symmetrical animal with conformation indicating power, endurance and agility and a look of intelligence and animation. The dog is neither unduly small nor conspicuously large. It gives the impression of medium size, but is like the proper hunter, "with a short back, but standing over plenty of ground." Symmetry and field quality are most essential. A dog in hard and lean field condition is not to be penalized; however, overly fat or poorly muscled dogs are to be penalized. A dog well balanced in all points is preferable to one with outstanding good qualities and defects. Grace of outline, clean-cut head, sloping shoulders, deep

Photo Courtesy of Taylor Harmon

CHAPTER 2   About the Breed

Photo Courtesy of Jenna Stankiewicz

chest, powerful back, strong quarters, good bone composition, adequate muscle, well carried tail and taut coat produce a look of nobility and indicate a heritage of purposefully conducted breeding. Further evidence of this heritage is movement which is balanced, alertly coordinated and without wasted motion.

Size, Proportion, Substance: Size- height of dogs, measured at the withers, 23 to 25 inches. Height of bitches, measured at the withers, 21 to 23 inches. Deviations of one inch above or below the described heights are to be severely penalized. Weight of dogs 55 to 70 pounds. Weight of bitches 45 to 60 pounds. Proportion- measuring from the forechest to the rearmost projection of the rump and from the withers to the ground, the Shorthair is permissibly either square or slightly longer than he is tall. Substance- thin and fine bones are by no means desirable in a dog which must possess strength and be able to work over any type of terrain. The main importance is not laid so much on the size of bone, but rather on the bone being in proper proportion to the body. Bone structure too heavy or too light is a fault. Tall and leggy dogs, dogs which are ponderous because of excess substance, doggy bitches, and bitchy dogs are to be faulted.

Head: The head is clean-cut, is neither too light nor too heavy, and is in proper proportion to the body. The eyes are of medium size, full of intelligence and expression, good-humored and yet radiating energy, neither protruding nor sunken. The eye is almond shaped, not circular. The preferred color is dark brown. Light yellow eyes are not desirable and are a

Photo Courtesy of Claire Holiday

fault. Closely set eyes are to be faulted. China or wall eyes are to be disqualified. The ears are broad and set fairly high, lie flat and never hang away from the head. Their placement is just above eye level. The ears when laid in front without being pulled, should extend to the corner of the mouth. In the case of heavier dogs, the ears are correspondingly longer. Ears too long or fleshy are to be faulted. The skull is reasonably broad, arched on the side and slightly round on top. Unlike the Pointer, the median line between the eyes at the forehead is not too deep and the occipital bone is not very conspicuous. The foreface rises gradually from nose to forehead. The rise is more strongly pronounced in the dog than in the bitch. The jaw is powerful and the muscles well developed. The line to the forehead rises gradually and never has a definite stop as that of the Pointer, but rather a stop-effect when viewed from the side, due to the position of the eyebrows. The muzzle is sufficiently long to enable the dog to seize game properly and be able to carry it for a long time. A pointed muzzle is not desirable. The depth is in the right proportion to the length, both in the muzzle and in the skull proper. The length of the muzzle should equal the length of skull. A dish-shaped muzzle is a fault. A definite Pointer stop is a serious fault. Too many wrinkles in the forehead is a fault. The nose is brown, the larger the better, and with nostrils well opened and broad. A spotted nose is not desirable. A flesh colored nose disqualifies. The chops fall away from the somewhat projecting nose. Lips are full and deep yet are never flewy. The teeth are strong and healthy. The molars intermesh properly. The bite is a true scissors bite. A perfect level bite is not desirable and must be penalized. Extreme overshot or undershot disqualifies.

Neck, Topline, Body: The neck is of proper length to permit the jaws reaching game to be retrieved, sloping downwards on beautifully curving lines. The nape is rather muscular, becoming gradually larger toward the shoulders. Moderate throatiness is permitted. The skin is close and tight. The chest in general gives the impression of depth rather than breadth; for all that, it is in correct proportion to the other parts of the body. The chest reaches down to the elbows, the ribs forming the thorax show a rib spring and are not flat or slabsided; they are not perfectly round or barrel-shaped. The back ribs reach well down. The circumference of the thorax immediately behind the elbows is smaller than that of the thorax about a hand's breadth behind elbows, so that the upper arm has room for movement. Tuck-up is apparent. The back is short, strong, and straight with a slight rise from the root of the tail to the withers. The loin is strong, is of moderate length, and is slightly arched. An excessively long, roached or swayed back must be penalized. The hips are broad with hip sockets wide apart and fall slightly toward the tail in a graceful curve. A steep croup is a fault. The tail is set high and firm, and must be docked, leaving approximately 40 percent of its length. The tail hangs down when the dog is quiet and is held horizontally when he is walking. The tail must never be curved over the back toward the head when the dog is moving. A tail curved or bent toward the head is to be severely penalized.

Forequarters: The shoulders are sloping, movable, and well covered with muscle. The shoulder blades lie flat and are well laid back nearing a 45-degree angle. The upper arm (the bones between the shoulder and elbow joint) is as long as possible, standing away somewhat from the trunk so that the straight and closely muscled legs, when viewed from the front, appear to be parallel. Elbows which stand away from the body or are too close result in toes turning inwards or outwards and must be faulted. Pasterns are strong, short and nearly vertical with a slight spring. Loose, short-bladed or straight shoulders must be faulted. Knuckling over is to be faulted. Dewclaws on the forelegs may be removed. The feet are compact, close-knit and

Photo Courtesy of Carey Anderson

round to spoonshaped. The toes are sufficiently arched and heavily nailed. The pads are strong, hard and thick.

Hindquarters: Thighs are strong and well-muscled. Stifles are well bent. Hock joints are well angulated and strong with straight bone structure from hock to pad. Angulation of both stifle and hock joint is such as to achieve the optimal balance of drive and traction. Hocks turn neither in nor out. Cowhocked legs are a serious fault.

Coat: The hair is short and thick and feels tough to the hand; it is somewhat longer on the underside of the tail and the back edges of the haunches. The hair is softer, thinner and shorter on the ears and the head. Any dog with long hair in the body coat is to be severely penalized.

Color: The coat may be of solid liver or a combination of liver and white such as liver and white ticked, liver patched and white ticked, or liver roan. A dog with any area of black, red, orange, lemon or tan, or a dog solid white will be disqualified.

Gait: A smooth lithe gait is essential. It is to be noted that as gait increases from the walk to a faster speed, the legs converge beneath the body. The tendency to single track is desirable. The forelegs reach well ahead as if to pull in the ground without giving the appearance of a hackney gait. The hindquarters drive the back legs smoothly and with great power.

Temperament: The Shorthair is friendly, intelligent, and willing to please. The first impression is that of a keen enthusiasm for work without indication of nervous or flighty character.

Disqualifications: China or wall eyes. Flesh colored nose. Extreme overshot or undershot. A dog with any area of black, red, orange, lemon, or tan, or a dog solid white.

Age Expectancy

The lifespan of a German Shorthaired Pointer is typically 12-14 years. When taking on a puppy, you should consider whether your circumstances or health are likely to change over this period, as your GSP will continue to be active well into his senior years.

If you cannot be reasonably confident that your health or circumstances will not change over such a long period, consider adopting an older GSP from a shelter. This option is better suited to experienced dog owners because not only is the GSP a challenging breed, but shelter dogs may have additional behavioral problems that require an experienced home.

Inside the Home

Although the German Shorthaired Pointer was bred as a working dog, this doesn't mean his natural home is in a kennel. On the contrary, as mentioned in Chapter 1, the GSP was deliberately bred to be a household com-

Photo Courtesy of Darcie Shea

panion, and to return to the family home after the day's work, to live with the household, and guard the property.

It is because of his bond with his humans that the German Shorthaired Pointer likes to be around them all day, every day. Although this is not practical for most people, any absences from the home should only be for short periods with this breed, as GSPs are not suited to a home where both owners are out all day.

The GSP is highly energetic and boisterous, so in a confined space he may be a liability, especially around very young children or those in frail health. But the dogs are excellent with responsible older children. Chapter 5 discusses introducing your children to your new GSP.

If you are very house proud, you may have chosen a German Shorthaired Pointer because he will not leave long dog hairs around the house. This is true; however, he will leave copious short dog hairs on your soft furnishings, which can be just as challenging to remove. It is also important to note that just because the GSP has a short coat, he is not hypoallergenic, and therefore the breed is not suitable for allergy sufferers. The dogs shed constantly, and the dander in the coat is the allergen.

It is easy to disregard the importance of daily brushing when you have a shorthaired breed. However, keeping on top of this will make cleaning up easier in the long run. And your GSP will of course, bring a lot less mud and dirt into your house on his coat than a longer haired breed.

You can read more about preparing your home for your German Shorthaired Pointer in Chapter 5.

Outside the Home

The German Shorthaired Pointer is in his element outdoors, so never will you have a better excuse to get out and about than when you have a GSP awaiting his daily exercise!

You will need a good-sized, totally secure yard for your GSP, so that he can burn off energy throughout the day, but without the possibility of jumping out to go explore somewhere more exciting.

By nature, as a hunting dog, the GSP has a very strong prey drive. So, if you have a cat, rabbit, guinea pig, ferret, birds or chickens, this may not be the breed for you. You should also take extra care when walking your dog near livestock or wildlife, as his instincts might override his obedience training. Beware, a farmer is legally entitled to shoot any dog on his land worrying his livestock.

The German Shorthaired Pointer is a very trainable dog, and recall training is especially important for this breed, as in order to exercise his body and mind to its full extent, your dog needs plenty of opportunity to run off-leash. There are tips on recall training in Chapter 6. Once your GSP is reliably trained to respond to your commands, he can enjoy agility, flyball, obedience and falconry, all of which will allow him to exercise his intelligence, and not use any pent-up frustrations in destructive or unwanted behavior.

Photo Courtesy of Ryan Goddard

CHAPTER 2 About the Breed

Most GSPs also love to swim, so your dog will appreciate the opportunity to visit the ocean, lakes or streams. But be aware of fast currents or rip tides, as well as toxic blue-green algae that can form in still water.

Your German Shorthaired Pointer should be given every opportunity to fulfill his physical and mental needs outside the home, and then you will be able to enjoy the company of a satisfied dog that may even settle down for a well-earned rest at the end of the day!

CHAPTER 3
Behavior

The German Shorthaired Pointer was bred for all the characteristics that make him a great hunter – intelligence, athleticism, energy, a strong prey drive and loyal companionship. These qualities can either make or break the dog if he isn't destined to work. So, when a German Shorthaired Pointer is given up to a rescue organization on account of behavior problems, these are rarely due to character flaws, but are a result of a lack of understanding on the owner's part about the importance of working with the breed's attributes. The GSP is an intelligent, busy dog that needs a home where he can fulfill his natural behavior. When his talents are recognized and encouraged, he is never a bad dog, and will never feel the pain of disappointing those he loves unconditionally.

Temperament and Personality

Raising a German Shorthaired Pointer is similar to the challenge of raising an intelligent child. There will be trouble if your dog isn't given plenty to occupy his body and mind. The breed can be hyperactive and boisterous, which is ideal in a hunting context where a dog has plenty of open space and needs both energy and stamina to do his job. In the home, this high level of energy can be less desirable. The solution lies in embracing the breed's lively nature, by accepting that a GSP is better suited to living in a larger sized home, with young and active owners that don't have very young children or frail elderly people sharing the home, who could get hurt. In the right home, the GSP's vitality brings joy rather than frustration.

The GSP is known to be slow to mature, so his bouncy exuberance will be with him for years. Unlike most breeds that reach adulthood at a year, the GSP remains a puppy until he is at least two years old, and some dogs may never fully mature. So, it's unrealistic to expect that your dog will sit quietly in a corner, suppressing his natural need to be involved with everything his beloved people are doing.

Having said that, the German Shorthaired Pointer is bright and trainable, and his education should start as early as possible. For the first few weeks, the GSP's trainer is his mom, and he shouldn't be taken from the litter too early. But as soon as he is home, he is ready to learn. The GSP feels most secure

CHAPTER 3 Behavior

Photo Courtesy of Jessica Arredondo

when he knows the ground rules and his place in the home, and this should be taught with patient and gentle positive reinforcement. The breed is very sensitive and wants desperately to please. Your GSP will become stressed with harsh training methods and disapproval. But he does require consistent and loving instruction to help him understand all that's required of him.

The GSP has a short attention span, so his training sessions need to be short and interesting to keep him focused. He is also smart enough to respond enthusiastically to rewards, and will be keen to learn exactly how to keep them coming!

Because the GSP is such a smart dog, if his intelligence isn't focused from day one on learning the things that you want, he will direct it into picking up bad habits, so as the owner of a German Shorthaired Pointer, you always want to work with his abilities, rather than have them work against you!

As a breed that does everything in life with intensity, the GSP is also known for his obsessive love for his people. This can be very endearing, and is nothing but positive if you can commit to a lifetime of being a dog's constant companion. However, be aware that with this breed, separation anxiety can be an issue. To a good extent, it can be managed by teaching your

Photo Courtesy of Ashleigh Scialo

dog how to be left alone, as discussed in Chapter 6. But again, it is important to work with the breed rather than against it, so don't choose a German Shorthaired Pointer if you are going to be away from home a lot.

Although the GSP was bred to also guard the family home, this is more directed towards alerting to the presence of strangers, rather than attacking. The breed isn't naturally aggressive to humans, nor to other dogs. However, a GSP's natural prey drive can make him unreliable around other small mammals and birds, so it's up to owners to keep their GSP away from anything that looks like breakfast.

> **FUN FACT**
> **Breed Popularity**
>
> In 2018, the German Shorthaired Pointer was ranked ninth-most popular breed in America, according to the American Kennel Club. This ranking was up from tenth-most popular in 2017. As of 2020, GSPs remain the ninth-most popular breed in America.

Importance of Socialization

Early socialization is important for any dog, but especially for the GSP, because the dogs are sensitive and feel most secure when they understand what is expected of them and how to deal with new situations. Also, a GSP needs to know he is able to trust completely in his beloved owner.

During the first few weeks of his life, your GSP learned his earliest socialization skills while sharing a space with his littermates, interacting with them by playing, learning his place within the small pack, and being nurtured and disciplined by his mom.

As well as socializing with his own kind, the breeder will have handled your dog regularly to get him accustomed to human contact, and he will probably have been introduced to some sights and sounds that will be a part of his life when he leaves for his new home.

When you bring your German Shorthaired Pointer puppy home, it will be a big change for him. He is sure to be excited by his new surroundings and freedoms. However, your new dog will still have a lot to process. If you don't have other dogs, he will be away from his own kind for the first time. He'll have new people to bond with and will need to learn the house rules. Your new GSP will be in an unfamiliar place, and for a dog that relies so heavily on scent, it will be difficult to no longer be able to smell his mother

Photo Courtesy of John Heiner

or littermates. Bringing home a blanket or towel from the breeder to put in your dog's crate can help with this.

Giving your GSP a bit of quiet time to become accustomed to his new home is ideal in the first days, but as soon as your puppy has completed his first vaccinations, he should be given the opportunity to meet other dogs. When you first take your puppy to the vet for his health check and follow-up shots, it's a good opportunity to ask for details of local puppy classes. Puppies have their own special language and way of playing and interacting, so this is a great place to start, allowing your dog some continuity from the life he knew before, but broadening his experience to dogs of other breeds and temperaments, in a controlled environment.

There is more about introducing your new GSP to other dogs and children in Chapter 5.

By socializing your puppy from the earliest age, you are teaching him how to feel safe and secure, so that he grows into a confident dog that is reliable and friendly, and most importantly, happy.

CHAPTER 3 Behavior

Exercise Requirements

The German Shorthaired Pointer is an active dog, and as an adult will take as much exercise as you can give him! However, he shouldn't be over-exercised during his first 18 months, while his joints and bones are still developing. It can seem quite challenging to get the right balance with a dog as full of energy as a GSP, since you may feel tempted to exhaust your dog so that he settles down. But you can achieve this just as much by exercising his brain as his body. So, in the early months, it is best to concentrate on training sessions rather than long walks, as training will set your dog up for life, without risk of injury or disability due to damaged joints or spines.

Your GSP will enjoy burning off energy in your yard, which should be very securely fenced, as the breed is known to be highly capable of escaping!

He will also enjoy playing with other dogs in his puppy classes, or meeting up for puppy playdates with other dog owners in your yard or theirs.

As he grows, your dog will enjoy going out for walks in a secure environment until his recall is reliably in place. The early months are ideal for teaching leash walking, as your dog learns these skills best if taught from an

Photo Courtesy of Shannon and Ryan Hughes

early age, and leash walking also controls his activity. There is more about this in Chapter 6.

Chapter 6 also provides recall tips that you can work on with your GSP, even in your back yard, as the breed is ideally suited to long walks off-leash once he reaches maturity. This will exercise both his body and mind.

Once your GSP is fully grown and physically mature (as mentally, he will take longer to catch up!), an adult dog requires at least two hours of exercise a day, with as much off-leash time as possible. This is best split into two daily walks which do not have to be of equal length, as long as one of them allows your dog to let off steam and exercise all his natural behaviors. If

Photo Courtesy of Mariana Gonzalez

CHAPTER 3 Behavior

Photo Courtesy of Taylor Felger

your GSP is a working dog, he may meet his exercise requirement simply by being out with you, depending on his job. If you are an active person, your dog will be in his element going jogging, cycling or hiking with you, and will be an excellent pace setter!

Common Behavior Problems

Many behavior problems in GSPs stem from insufficient exercise or mental stimulation. The breed is a ball of energy that has to find its release somewhere, and if your dog is under-stimulated or expected to settle for a sedentary life, the stress he feels will lead him to become destructive.

A bored German Shorthaired Pointer will find ways to occupy himself, such as finding an escape route out of your yard. If he has not been given the attention he craves, his bond with his owner will not be as strong, and he will lose his instinct to please or his understanding of how to behave.

Most behavior problems with the GSP can be anticipated through understanding the breed's nature, and therefore either choosing a different breed better suited to the owner's lifestyle, or addressing potential behaviors right from the early weeks. For example, the GSP has a strong prey drive, but a puppy brought up with a cat will usually accept it, even if he has less tolerance for the neighbor's cats.

The breed also suffers badly from separation anxiety, but if he is taught to be left alone from an early age, he may tolerate it for short periods. Training to prevent separation anxiety is further discussed in Chapter 6.

GSPs are not known to be excessive barkers, but if they are left alone for long periods, this could become a problem. Again, it is a matter of only choosing the breed if you can be with your dog most of the time.

As a busy dog, prone to boredom, the GSP can be destructive, especially in his younger years. All puppies chew to relieve the discomfort of their teeth coming through, and to explore their new world, but as your GSP gets older, his chewing may become even more destructive. Usually he will grow out of the tendency for random destruction around the age of two or three, but in the meantime, you will need to outsmart him. From the get-go, anything of importance or value should be removed from the reach of your dog, and the doors closed on rooms to which he isn't allowed access. His

Photo Courtesy of Cassidy Flanagan

chewing instincts should then be directed to acceptable things, such as indestructible toys, and chews such as antlers that will not splinter or break. If you catch your dog chewing something he shouldn't, remove it from him, or remove the dog from the item if it is the furniture, and give him a permitted chew instead. Your GSP is a smart dog and will get the message eventually.

The breed can also be prone to dominance. The GSP finds security in the concept of a pack order, but he needs to understand that his place is not at the top. He tends to respect his owner as pack leader, however, he may dominate other household members and challenge them for his place higher up the chain. Involving your children with training, feeding and exercising your dog will show him that his place is at the bottom of the pack. Your GSP should not be allowed privileges such as sleeping on a bed, as this encourages him to think he is next in the hierarchy, and he may then snap at those he sees as beneath him.

Whereas most problem behaviors can be avoided by early training, if you are adopting an older GSP, he may already have ingrained issues, and these are much harder to deal with. Involving a trained behaviorist is a good idea when taking on a rescue dog. Often the rescue organization will have a behaviorist that they use and who will be able to give advice, or recommend another professional in your area. However experienced you are with dogs in general, it can be reassuring to have expert guidance in addressing the particular issues your GSP may be facing, and helping him to overcome his fears and thrive in his new home.

CHAPTER 4
How to Choose a German Shorthaired Pointer

Purchasing or Rescuing?

If you have considered all the pros and cons of owning a German Shorthaired Pointer, and are ready for the craziness of the ride, you may now be considering if you should purchase a puppy, or adopt an unwanted GSP from a shelter.

It has already been mentioned that the GSP is not an ideal dog for first-time owners. So, with this breed more than most, adopting an older dog that may have ingrained behavior issues should be left for those with previous experience of the breed. In fact, many specialist GSP rescues will only

Photo Courtesy of Michele Hierholzer

CHAPTER 4 How to Choose a German Shorthaired Pointer

Photo Courtesy of Brandi Rausch

adopt out their dogs to experienced homes. However, not all GSPs in rescue will have behavior problems; some will have been handed in simply due to a change in circumstances, so they may be well trained and well adjusted. If you are lucky enough to find such a dog in need of a loving home, this option could suit anyone wishing to bypass the puppy stage, or who feels particularly drawn to the deep satisfaction rescuing a dog brings.

If you have owned dogs before, but this is your first GSP, buying from a Kennel Club registered breeder is an excellent choice. There are also other organizations which breeders can register with if they have working dogs, and these are discussed further in Chapter 7.

The GSP is a beautiful and multi-talented dog, and this is why people are drawn to the breed. So, you may wish to show your dog or compete in field trials. If so, you will usually need to buy from a breeder. This is because

Photo Courtesy of Stephen and Stacia Heintz

CHAPTER 4 How to Choose a German Shorthaired Pointer

show dogs have to have pedigree papers. Rescue dogs do not always come with papers, even if they were handed in with them. This is both to give the dog a fresh start and to protect the anonymity of the previous owner. Additionally, most rescues will spay or neuter their dogs before rehoming them, so that they are not used for breeding or profit. Neutered dogs cannot compete in Kennel Club shows in the United States, although in the UK it is possible to show a neutered dog with a special exemption certificate. However, if you only wish to take part in local fun shows, then you will not usually need a pedigree certificate, and neither will it make a difference if your dog is neutered or not.

> **CELEBRITY DOGS**
> **Andy Williams**
>
> Legendary singer Andy Williams was a lifelong dog lover, in addition to being a Grammy-nominated performer with multiple gold- and platinum-certified records. At least two of Williams' dogs were German Shorthaired Pointers. These GSPs, Cody and Sophie, appeared alongside their owner on the cover of Palm Springs Life magazine in 1997.

If you are more inclined to competing in activity trials, some classes such as AKC Working Trials, Agility and Obedience are open to all dogs, as long as they are registered on the Activity Register. However, to compete in Field Trials, Tests and Gundog Trials, you will need a registered pedigree and enrollment on the Breed Register, so this may affect your choice of breeder or rescue.

Other reasons for choosing a breeder may be because you have seen and admired a GSP belonging to a friend or acquaintance, and have asked them where their dog came from. All breeders have their own special stamp on the dogs they produce, so finding a dog in prime health and with a winning temperament is a good indicator that the breeder is producing from excellent bloodlines. This means you are taking on a known quantity, as far as it is possible to do so.

In adopting a GSP, you can only go by what you see. However, the rescue will fully assess dogs before matching them to their new homes, as well as giving them a full vet check and dealing with any health issues. A different scenario is when a dog is purchased from a private advertisement, or "free-to-a-good-home," in which case there may be all sorts of problems ahead, and the purchaser should go in with their eyes wide open to what they may be letting themselves in for.

Photo Courtesy of Jake and Nicolette Arnitz

If you want to hunt with your German Shorthaired Pointer, you may have a good idea of the bloodlines you are looking for, and the breeders that produce proven hunting partners. In that case, this is an excellent reason to buy a puppy from a breeder, with the added incentive of training the dog yourself for his job, and building your bond along the way. Chapter 7 further discusses how to choose a puppy for hunting. But it is because of his hunting instinct and energy that the GSP often finds himself being surrendered, because he was purchased by a family that was not prepared for the qualities that make him so talented in the field, but such a livewire in the home! So, if you are experienced with working dogs, you may find your ideal hunting partner in a shelter, and for your dog, all his Christmases will

CHAPTER 4 How to Choose a German Shorthaired Pointer

have come early! Just remember, a hunting dog should ideally be trained from a puppy, so if your rescue GSP is destined for hunting, do not expect training to be simple.

When you take on a dog, especially a GSP that bonds so closely with his special people, it is a commitment for the lifetime of the dog. So, for some people who cannot say how their health or circumstances might change over the next 12 years or so, adopting an older dog makes sense. And as long as you can be fairly sure you will remain active enough for the needs of a GSP, this can be a good alternative to taking on a puppy. Not all GSPs in rescue have behavioral or emotional needs; some will have been handed over for other reasons, such as the death of their previous owner, a new baby, or a family moving to rented accommodations where dogs are not allowed. So, for active seniors without work commitments, adopting a GSP can bring a lot of joy and satisfaction all round.

Male or Female?

The most fundamental question, when you have decided to get a German Shorthaired Pointer, is whether to get a male or a female dog. It's very much a personal choice. But if your mind is not already made up, there are certain considerations that might help you choose what's best for you.

To start with, if you already have a dog in the home, as a general rule, it is best to get a second dog of the opposite gender, as long as at least one of them is neutered. Relationships between dogs of the opposite gender are generally more harmonious. If you do choose two dogs of the same sex, two males will usually get on better than two females, although they may be more boisterous. This is because two females can compete if they are both dominant. If one is more submissive, however, two females can get along fine.

Dominance can be an issue with the German Shorthaired Pointer, with the female being generally more dominant than the male.

If you don't already have a dog, then your choice of male or female comes down to what works best for you.

Firstly, a male dog will grow slightly bigger than a female. He may also have a chunkier appearance, although the GSP as a breed is slender. The difference in size and build is unlikely to matter much in the decision process.

More significant is the difference in sex hormones. Until your dog is castrated in the case of a male, or spayed if she is female, you will notice some distinct differences once your dog reaches sexual maturity.

The most significant is that your female dog will start to come into season twice a year, and for two to three weeks she will drip blood, which can be messy and smelly. She will also be extremely attractive to unneutered male dogs, so your dog cannot be walked in public areas during this time. For this reason, most owners of female GSPs choose to spay their dog if they do not wish to breed her. Spaying also protects against certain cancers and a uterine condition called pyometra, although it can affect your dog's coat.

Male dogs also undergo changes at sexual maturity, and may start to mark their territory, mount other dogs, and be more inclined to roam. To prevent these undesirable behaviors, and to save him from fathering any unwanted litters, it is wise to castrate your male dog. This is cheaper and simpler than spaying a female. Spaying and neutering are further discussed in Chapter 12.

With a friendly dog such as the GSP, aggression is rarely an issue. So, the common perception that males are more aggressive than females needn't figure much in the equation, bearing in mind that any dog may bite if provoked or taken by surprise.

Likewise, there is little difference in trainability between the sexes. Males may be more easily distracted, but they make up for it with strategic thinking. Many trainers prefer one particular sex for their working dog, but this is generally down to personal preference as both can be found in the field.

So, whatever your choice, you are unlikely to go wrong, as long as you have thought about their health issues, and what is involved in their care.

Researching the Establishment

In narrowing down your choice of breeder, the first important distinction is between a show breeder and a working breeder. If you plan to hunt with your GSP, buy a dog from strong working lines. If you plan to show your dog, or you just want a family dog, then a puppy bred from winning show stock will make an ideal companion.

If you already know a bit about GSP bloodlines, or you are looking to buy a puppy from the same breeder as a friend's dog that you admire, you may already have a specific kennels in your sights. It is important to accept

CHAPTER 4 How to Choose a German Shorthaired Pointer

Photo Courtesy of Alice Sharp & Joel Mullan

that if this breeder's dogs are in demand, you may have to go on a wait list for a puppy, and sometimes you may have to put down a deposit.

    If you do not know of a specific breeder, or feel that the wait will be too long, the best place to find a list of Kennel Club registered breeders is on the Kennel Club website for your country. You can then research the breeders that are within the radius you are prepared to travel, to see how their dogs have fared in shows and working trials. By choosing to buy from a Kennel Club registered breeder, you have the peace of mind that the dogs are being produced from healthy parents with good temperaments, the parents are fully screened for genetic conditions, the mother is not overbred, conditions are clean and safe, your dog will come with pedigree papers, health certificates and Kennel Club registration, and you will have full breeder support and a returns policy if anything should not go to plan.

Nevertheless, any reputable breeder will not object to you visiting his premises yourself to check the conditions, and the quality of his dogs.

If you choose instead to buy from a hobby breeder, you have none of these guarantees, and should be aware that puppy farms are not always obvious to the inexperienced purchaser. Often when a purchaser responds to an advertisement in the newspaper or online from someone that has a litter available, they will make an appointment to view the dogs in the clean front room of a family house, whereas the dogs' true living conditions may be in squalid and overcrowded kennels or sheds that no purchaser ever sees. The parents or the pup, unless microchipped, may not correspond to the paperwork, and unless both parents are Kennel Club registered, it will not be possible to register the puppy, so a showing career will not be open to him.

Puppies purchased from amateur breeders are also much more likely to suffer from health problems, which may be apparent right from the start, or further down the line. This is because the parents are not selected rigorously from only the best of their breed. The parents of unregistered litters are also unlikely to have gone through expensive health screening, and may have been bred at too young or elderly an age, without observation of the recommended intervals between litters.

So, a cheap GSP puppy may cost you a great deal more financially over his lifetime, as well as the cost in stress and heartbreak if he has health or character issues.

Also, as a purchaser who cares for the health and welfare of the German Shorthaired Pointer, and dogs in general, there is a moral aspect to supporting responsible breeding, and steering clear of the financial exploitation of dogs in the breeding market, at the expense of their welfare.

Finally, if you are not purchasing a puppy, but have decided instead to offer a home to a GSP in rescue, you may think that researching the establishment isn't applicable to your situation. However, just as there are excellent breeders, and ones to avoid, the same applies to rescue organizations. Most dog rescue organizations and shelters are regulated and run to very high standards, with only the best interests of the dogs in mind. A bit of online research usually reveals the reputation of the rescue organization.

If you are planning to rescue a GSP, the best place to start is with a rescue specializing in the German Shorthaired Pointer. Failing that, you may find a general Pointer rescue or a gundog rescue. These organizations have

CHAPTER 4   How to Choose a German Shorthaired Pointer

the best understanding of this complex breed, and are in the best position to assess their dogs and place them in the best-matched homes. Along with other reputable all-breed rescues, you can expect your dog to be assessed, vet-checked, neutered, vaccinated, dewormed, have had parasite control treatment, to be microchipped, and to come with a contract between you and the rescue. You will also be expected to have a home check, even if you already have dogs or previous experience of the breed. You can also expect to pay a substantial rehoming fee that goes some way to covering your dog's costs in the rescue.

If you are not given evidence that your dog has received this level of care, it should serve as a warning that the rescue may be profiteering. A reputable rescue will also make it a condition of rehoming that if your circumstances change, your dog should be returned to the rescue and not passed on by yourself. This is to guarantee the dog's future, so that his home will always be approved by the rescue, and he is not taken for the wrong reasons and sold for profit.

Inquire About the Parents and Health Tests

When you have identified a breeder that either has a litter available, or is expecting one in the near future, he will not be at all averse to answering lots of questions from you. In fact, good breeders will welcome questions, as it shows that the prospective owner is taking the responsibility seriously. And every good breeder wants the best home for their puppies, so don't be surprised if you are asked lots of questions too!

GSPs can be subject to certain inherited conditions for which both parents should be tested, so you should ask the breeder about which health tests he carries out on his breeding stock.

In the US, you should expect the following certification for both parents of a German Shorthaired Pointer:

- A certificate from the Canine Eye Registry Foundation (CERF) – dated within the past year – certifying the dog to be free of eye diseases, including a DNA test for Progressive Retinal Atrophy (PRA).
- A certificate from the Orthopedic Foundation of America (OFA) or PennHip certifying the dog to have normal hips. Hip scores range from 0 to 106 (53 on each hip). It is expressed as two numbers, and the lower the score the better. Breeders should only be breeding from parents that score below the breed average, and for a GSP, this is 10, or 5:5. As well as a low number, you should be looking for even numbers on both sides.

- A certificate from the Orthopedic Foundation of America (OFA) certifying the dog to have normal elbows. Elbow scores are rated 0-3. 0 is a perfect elbow, so both parents should score 0.
- A certificate from the Orthopedic Foundation of America (OFA) or a report from a veterinary cardiologist – dated within the past year – certifying that the dog has had an Advanced Cardiac Examination and has a normal heart.

Additionally, at least one parent should have a DNA test proving they are clear of a severe hereditary eye disease called Cone Degeneration (CD2), and a bleeding disorder called von Willebrand's disease (VWDII), both of which may be found in the GSP. These are recessive genes, but if you ever intend to breed from your dog, both parents should be tested clear of these conditions or your puppy may be a carrier.

Some registered breeders will also have additional DNA tests carried out on their breeding dogs, but is important to realize that the GSP can suffer from many more conditions for which tests are not available, so you should ask the breeder about the medical history of the parents, grandparents and great-grandparents. Conditions to be aware of include the following:

- Atopy
- Cancer (mammary carcinoma, nasal carcinoma, mast cell tumor, lipoma)
- Cherry eye
- Cutaneous lupus erythematosus
- Dermatitis
- Entropion
- GM2 gangliosidosis
- Hemophilia
- Heart disease: Subaortic stenosis
- Hemivertebrae
- Idiopathic epilepsy
- Lipoma
- Myasthenia gravis
- Osteochondritis dissecans (OCD)
- Panosteitis
- Polyarthritis/meningitis syndrome

You should ask the breeder about their policy if any genetic conditions should affect your dog later in life, as a good breeder will be keen to know about this, in order to inform his breeding decisions. He may also agree to a contribution towards medical costs or a refund of the purchase price.

You should ask to see a copy of the parents' pedigrees, and you should look for as little inbreeding as possible across at least 5 generations. This is because there is a greater risk of inherited diseases where the same names crop up multiple times in a dog's pedigree. The GSP has a small gene pool, so is at risk of inbreeding, therefore it is something to look out for. Your breeder may be able to provide the COI score for his litter, which stands for Coefficient of Inbreeding. For the GSP, the average COI for a GSP across 5 generations is 5.3% (UK Kennel Club 2020). If your pup's score is significantly higher, it is not necessarily something to worry about, as long as the parents and grandparents are healthy.

A good breeder should take the greatest care of his breeding females. The mother should be between the age of two and eight years at the time of whelping. You should also check that she has had no more than one litter in a 12-month period, and no more than three litters in her lifetime.

Ask the breeder about after-sales support. A good breeder will remain invested in the welfare of his puppies, and always be willing to be contacted for advice and support. Some will even offer vacation boarding. Most reputable breeders will take a puppy back if things don't work out, or you are no longer able to care for it.

Looking at the Puppy

Going to see the litter of puppies for the first time is an exciting moment, and you may have visions of an instant connection between yourself and your new soul mate. Sometimes this happens, and that's great, as your relationship with your dog is all about the bond. But for those looking for a more scientific approach to choosing the best puppy for them, there are certain things to look out for.

To start with, it is not always easy to differentiate between puppies in a litter, as they should all be lively, healthy and confident. When you meet the litter, you should always be able to meet the mother, who may still be suckling her puppies, depending on when you first meet them. You may or may not be able to meet the father, as not all breeders will use their own male dogs, and it is often a good sign for genetic diversity if the father has come from a different kennels; however, you should be able to see photographs of him.

It is only by looking at the parents that you can predict how the puppies will turn out. Even their markings will change as they get older, with ticking and roaning appearing if the parents have these traits. Solid color patches, however, will characterize the dog throughout its life, and you may feel particularly drawn to how some of these defining markings appear on your chosen puppy. There is nothing shallow in choosing a puppy for his looks if you are buying from a registered breeder with a litter of well-bred puppies in prime health, as every pup should grow to be the best of his breed.

Photo Courtesy of Jessica Arredondo

There may, however, be subtle character differences between the puppies in the litter if you are patient and observe them for long enough. Some will be more assertive, and others more shy. If you are not instinctively drawn to either end of the spectrum, a good policy is to select a puppy from midway between the extremes, if you do not want to have to deal with either dominance or fearfulness.

You may find that the breeder recommends a puppy to you, based on what he has learned from your discussions, and which of his puppies he thinks will be the best match for you. It is certainly worth taking his advice, because the breeder knows his puppies best, and it is in his best interests for the partnership to work out. He is deeply invested in the future welfare of his dogs, and on a more practical note, taking a puppy back later on will be disruptive for the dog, and will be harder for the breeder to sell on.

You should watch the breeder pick up the puppies in turn. They should be relaxed and accepting of being handled. You may then be given the opportunity to pick up the pups yourself to check their physical health. There are several things you should be looking for when selecting your puppy, and the American Kennel Club lists these as follows:

- The skin should not have parasites, hair loss, crusts or reddened areas.
- The eyes, ears, and nose should be free of crusts and discharge.
- The nostrils should be wide and open.
- None of the puppies should be coughing, sneezing, or vomiting.
- The area around the anus should have no hint of irritation or recent diarrhea.
- Puppies should be neither thin nor pot-bellied.
- The gums should be pink, not pale.
- The eyelids and lashes should not fold in on the eyes.

CHAPTER 4   How to Choose a German Shorthaired Pointer

- By the age of 12 weeks, males should have both testicles descended into the scrotum. Undescended testicles have a greater chance of becoming cancerous, and neutering such dogs is more involved.
- Avoid any puppy that is making significant breathing sounds, including excessive wheezing or snorting.
- Puppies should not be limping or lethargic. If they are, ask to see them again the next day in case it is a temporary limp, or the puppy is simply sleepy.

(Source: AKC Canine Health Foundation)

When you pick up your puppy, he should come with a comprehensive puppy pack, containing your contract of sale, your dog's registration certificate and pedigree, immunization record, worming record, and advice for continuation of care, socialization, exercise and training. You will also receive a contractual guarantee, detailing any conditions that may apply if you need to return a puppy. The contract may involve a considerable amount of paperwork, so be prepared to spend some time going through it before signing.

As soon as possible after collecting your puppy, you should take him to your vet for a full physical examination. This will make sure you haven't missed anything that may affect the health of your GSP. It will also get him registered with your vet for the continuation of his vaccinations and health care. If the vet should pick up any serious issue at this first examination, you should not delay in returning your puppy to the breeder before forming a deep attachment. Happily, this is a rare occurrence and through diligent selection of your puppy, he should sail through his first vet check with flying colors, ready to start his new life!

Considerations of a Rescue Dog

As previously mentioned, German Shorthaired Pointers may come into rescue because their family is unable to cope with the breed. This may be due to the fact they underestimated how bouncy and often demanding the GSP is by nature, or they were not prepared for this to be magnified tenfold by the challenges of puppyhood. None of these factors are the fault of the dog, although depending how long a dog had been with his owners before they gave up on him, he may have missed out on those precious early weeks of formative training. So, you may find a very well-bred GSP in a shelter, who just has to catch up on his learning. And if you have previous experience with dogs, you may feel up to the challenge.

Sadly, sometimes a GSP will find his way into rescue after a longer period of neglect or cruelty, in which case he will have psychological baggage that requires considerable experience of the breed. Rescue organizations often have their own behaviorist to help the new owner work with their dog to overcome ingrained behaviors and learn to trust again.

Other times, an older dog may be handed over to the shelter when his owner dies or due to a change in circumstances. So, there are many different temperaments and life stages of GSP in your nation's shelters, and you may find a soul mate that matches exactly what you have to offer.

It is always worth looking for a specialist German Shorthaired Pointer Rescue or gundog rescue for the most knowledgeable support, and greatest choice of dogs. A good rescue will take an ongoing interest in how their dog gets on in his new home, and will always be there to offer advice. Also, you will sign a contract to agree that if your circumstances change, you will return the dog to the rescue for rehoming, a policy known as Rescue Backup.

Public shelters offer a whole range of dogs, but you may find a GSP in a shelter near you. In the US, Canada and Mexico, a good starting point is the website www.petfinder.com.

When you have found a dog and have sent in your application, you can expect to have a home check. This is to confirm your address and identity, but also for the rescue to be sure you understand the implications of taking on a dog, and have a suitable home to welcome the new arrival.

You may have already met your dog if you have found him in a local shelter, but sometimes you will only have seen him online, as many rescues house their dogs in foster homes rather than kennels. So, after you have passed your home check, you may be invited to a 'meet and greet' to meet your new dog. This is especially important if you already have a dog, and should take place on neutral territory when the two dogs first meet.

When you bring home your rescue dog, especially if he is an adult whose world has been turned upside down, you should give him lots of quiet time to settle. This may take months, so it is important to be patient. Most dogs are adaptable, and soon imprint on their new provider, so before long your dog will have forgotten his past, and be ready to take on his future as part of his new family. If this takes a little longer than you expect, give your dog all the time he needs, as further upheavals will only set him back further. Remember the rescue is always there to help, and if you need further support, the GSP society in your country is another knowledgeable resource.

Reasons for Not Choosing a German Shorthaired Pointer

It should be apparent by now that the GSP thrives in a home with young, active adults. He will also thrive when living with fit seniors who have an outdoor lifestyle, and his friendly nature will make him a great friend to older children.

You should look for a different breed, or maybe think carefully about whether owning a dog is for you if:

- You are at work all day and your dog will be left on his own. Even employing a dog walker to visit at lunch time is no substitute for the day-long human company that the GSP craves.
- You have young children who are crawling or unsteady on their feet, or not mature enough to understand how to behave around a large, exuberant, sensitive dog. Or you expect to welcome a baby in the foreseeable future.
- You are not fit and active, unless you can employ a dog walker to take care of your GSP's considerable daily exercise needs, and you can provide companionship throughout the rest of the day.
- You or anyone in your home is frail or unsteady on their feet, as your GSP is excitable and has very little spatial awareness!
- You do not have your own safely enclosed yard where your GSP can let off steam between his longer walks, to alleviate boredom and for his toileting needs.
- You do not live near open countryside that can be accessed daily on foot or by car.
- You are excessively bothered by hair, dirt or doggy odor, or someone in the home has allergies.
- Your circumstances are likely to change within the lifespan of your dog (as far as it is possible to predict).

If you do not fall into any of these categories, and are ready for your life never to be the same, then things are about to get a whole lot crazier, busier and full of fun when you bring home your German Shorthaired Pointer!

CHAPTER 5
Preparations for a New Dog

Whether you are buying a German Shorthaired Pointer puppy from a breeder, or adopting your dog from a shelter or rescue organization, there will usually be a few weeks between reserving your dog and bringing him home, and this is your opportunity to make sure everything is in place to welcome your new arrival.

Photo Courtesy of Anna AL-Shishani

CHAPTER 5 Preparations for a New Dog

Preparing the Outside of Your House

Your German Shorthaired Pointer is a livewire, and in between his walks he will be spending a lot of time in your yard, burning off energy and keeping his body and mind occupied! So, your yard is a good place to start when preparing your home for your new dog.

If you already have a dog, you may think you can skip this stage, as your resident dog doesn't get into trouble in the yard or try to escape. However, your GSP will come with a whole new set of behaviors and escape methods that your resident dog probably grew out of long ago, or never thought of in the first place! Also, if your resident dog is small or not particularly athletic, he won't need six-foot fences to keep him in, but your German Shorthaired Pointer certainly will. You may not pay much attention to the gaps under the fences or broken fence panels, but your GSP puppy will certainly find them.

> **FUN FACT**
> **Gaming and GSPs**
>
> Hunting Simulator 2, a PC game released by the French video game company Nacon in 2020, is designed to be a realistic simulation of hunting. Your character begins the game with a beagle puppy and is later able to upgrade to a German Shorthaired Pointer. GSPs, prized for their hunting abilities in real life, perform tasks for your character in the game, including tracking prey, distracting big game, retrieving kills, and pointing in the direction of a detected animal for your character.

Bear in mind too, that until your male GSP is neutered, he will have a strong roaming instinct as he reaches sexual maturity. So, until your new GSP understands the physical boundaries of his new territory, and is bonded with you, has learned obedience, and knows what is expected of him, his natural curiosity and instincts to roam need to be anticipated, and your yard made totally GSP-secure (which is one grade up from dog-secure!).

Also, a German Shorthaired Pointer is a valuable pedigree dog and a target for dog thieves. So, you should make sure your back gate is locked at all times, and if your gate doesn't have a lock, attach one before you bring your dog home.

If you are adopting a dog, you probably have had a home check, and any shortcomings in your yard's security will have been brought to your attention. If these were major, such as incomplete or insufficiently high fencing, the home checker may need to come back to make sure this has been remedied before your dog comes home. It's in your interest to make absolutely

Photo Courtesy of Aaron Retzlaff

CHAPTER 5   Preparations for a New Dog

sure the home checker didn't miss any other escape routes or hazards by doing your own thorough checks, especially if your boundary is extensive.

A boundary check isn't something you do just once before your dog arrives. It should be a regular habit, especially if your dog digs or there are other wild animals in your area that may tunnel under your fence. And always check your fences after high winds.

It's up to you whether you wish your dog to have full access to your yard, or whether you wish to divide off an area for him. There may be several reasons for dividing your yard:

- You have children, who need a safe and clean area to play in.
- You are a keen gardener and want to have a part of your yard where plants can grow undisturbed, or simply a tranquil area for relaxation.
- You have potential hazards in your yard, such as toxic plants, a greenhouse, garden pond, shingle, building materials or other items that could be harmful or poisonous, such as garage chemicals like antifreeze. There are hundreds of plants which can be potentially toxic to dogs, and a comprehensive list can be found on the ASPCA's Poison Control website: https://www.aspca.org/pet-care/animal-poison-control/toxic-and-non-toxic-plants
- You have chickens or small animals – in which case any partitions should be both solid and extra-secure, as a GSP has a very high prey drive.

Bear in mind that in the yard area where your dog is allowed, he will play, dig and potty. Playing may either be with you or on his own, in which case any toys left out should be indestructible. Digging may be destructive, or may compromise the security of your boundary, so providing a permitted digging area often works to contain your dog's version of a game. A sandpit, or partly buried toys can help your dog recognize the area where he is allowed to dig. As for toileting, you may find your dog has his own favorite areas, and you should have a poop-scoop ready to clear up his mess every day.

If you are going to leave your GSP in the yard for any period of time, for example when you are out the house, he will need a comfy kennel, a water bowl and some toys to play with. Inside his kennel, you should place a warm bed or pillows and blankets to ensure that he doesn't become cold. Your GSP is better suited as an indoor dog, due to his thin coat, but can be left outside when you are out for a few hours if necessary.

Preparing the Inside of Your House

You may also have to manage your expectations inside the home. If you haven't had a dog before, it's important to realize that dirt, odor and dog hair come with dog ownership, and even if you aren't ready to fully embrace it, you can manage it to some extent and still maintain a hygienic home.

If you're bringing home a puppy, one thing you can be sure of is that there will be potty-training accidents. Potty training is covered in Chapter 6; however, it is a process, and your GSP puppy does not yet have full physical

Photo Courtesy of Sydney Zamago

CHAPTER 5 Preparations for a New Dog

Photo Courtesy of Melissa Moore

control of his bladder and bowels, so in the first few weeks and months, you will occasionally be cleaning the floor.

If you have hard floors in your home, this is a definite advantage, as cleaning up thoroughly after your puppy is quick and easy. If, however, you have carpets, you should consider now whether you wish your puppy to have access to your carpeted rooms. If not, you may section them off with stair gates, or simply close the doors on them. If you're more relaxed about your dog accessing your carpeted rooms, a carpet shampooing machine is a worthwhile investment, enabling you to spot-clean any accidents without leaving any odor. This is important, as dogs are drawn back to areas that have been soiled previously. When cleaning up after your dog, you should use an enzymatic cleaner that breaks down the ammonia component of your dog's urine.

When you have decided which rooms your dog is going to be allowed into, look for and remove any hazards. Puppies love to chew. Remove any objects with batteries, such as the TV remote, children's toys, valuables and medicines. Bear in mind, foods such as chocolate, raisins and chewing gum can be toxic to dogs, so be sure everyone in the family knows not to leave their snacks lying around. Also consider that if your dog is going to be left unsupervised, he may start chewing larger objects such as the furniture or rugs, so any expensive items may be best moved to another room or into storage until your GSP is older. The bathroom should also always be out of bounds to your GSP, as he may get into your drugs cabinet or come into contact with bleach or toilet cleaners if left to explore by himself. Finally, remember your GSP is a very lively, bouncy character, so be sure to clear a space for him, and remove anything breakable from floor level.

When planning where your dog will be allowed, you also need to consider where he will sleep. Given the choice, your GSP will almost certainly want to sleep in your room, on your bed! Not only is this a hard habit to

Photo Courtesy of Casey Yager

CHAPTER 5 Preparations for a New Dog

break, but it can be unhygienic with a dog that is not yet potty trained, or a female in heat, as well as creating dominance problems. So, from day one, it's important that your dog learns to settle in his own bed. This should not be in the bedroom, but depending on the layout of your home, may be in the kitchen, hallway or living room, as long as it's out of drafts. And the best way of ensuring your dog stays in his own bed overnight is to crate train him from the very beginning. Not only does crate training help with potty training, but it creates a safe space for your dog where he learns to settle. This has benefits for your dog's emotional health, and has many practical benefits for your life as a dog owner.

German Shorthaired Pointers are one of the most affectionate dog breeds, and for many people the main attraction is the idea of cuddles on the couch. However, your GSP's idea of cuddles on the couch may involve you getting jumped on, trampled, and licked to death! If this is for you, then your dog will take any amount of it, but be ready for the dog hair that will stick to all the soft furnishings as well as your clothes! If you have leather upholstery, this is easier to clean than fabric, although it is likely to get scratched. Throws are a good way to protect your furniture. Most GSP owners find a good quality vacuum cleaner with upholstery attachments to be a very worthwhile investment. And a lint roller will save your clothes, since your GSP has dark hairs for your light clothes and light hairs for your dark clothes, so hairs will always be visible.

There are several perfectly good reasons why you may not wish your GSP to get on the couch. Apart from the hair, dirt and damage, you may not want your dog hassling your visitors when they are trying to sit down. If you have children, it is also wise to make the couch off-limits to prevent dominance issues. If you don't want your GSP on the couch, it may be a challenge with this breed, but you need to be totally consistent. This means even if you are out, your dog should not have access to the couch, as flouting the rule when you are not there to enforce it gives your dog a sense of one-upmanship, and he can become dominant. So, your dog would need to be confined to his crate, the kitchen, or the yard when you are not around.

In thinking well ahead during the weeks leading up to your dog's homecoming, you can preempt any problems before they occur, so your dog slots in right away, and you are well prepared for every eventuality!

Shopping List

If you already have a dog, or have had one in the past and still have some of his things, your shopping list for your new GSP will be shorter than for those who will be welcoming their first dog. If you're in new territory, the array of things for sale in the pet store can seem overwhelming. But most of these things are luxuries that you can choose whether or not to buy later. To begin with, you just need a few basics.

Crates

If you are buying a puppy, crate training him from the get-go is an excellent idea. It will help with his potty training, give him some structure in understanding when to settle, give him a safe space that he can call his own, keep him under control if visitors or children come to the house, and the crate is a bit of home for him when you travel. If you ever need to board your dog with friends or pet sitters, they will also greatly appreciate a crate trained dog. Crate training improves both your life and your dog's.

If you are adopting a rescue dog, depending on his age and past experiences, crate training may or may not be an option. Your rescue organization will be able to advise you on your particular dog. But a crate is still useful to have for travel, and in case your dog should ever need crate rest for illness or injury. So, it is advisable to accustom your older dog to a crate by leaving the door open so that he can come and go at will, but make it comfortable and interesting for him, by putting bedding and toys inside, or even feeding him in his crate.

There are several types of crates. Airline standard crates are the strongest, but unless you intend to take your dog anywhere by air, you will not need to invest in one of these. Fabric crates are lightweight and can seem cozier than metal crates, but your GSP is likely to destroy one of these very quickly. A sturdy, collapsible metal crate is your best bet for your German Shorthaired Pointer. Look for one with a metal tray rather than plastic, because your GSP may turn out to be a chewer.

When it comes to size, your GSP puppy will grow into quite a large dog; however, he does not need the biggest size crate to begin with. This is because when potty training your dog, he is naturally disinclined to soil his sleeping area, but in an extra-large crate he may soil the opposite corner, whereas you want to encourage him to toilet when he is let out of the crate. So, a medium crate is ideal to start with.

CHAPTER 5 Preparations for a New Dog

You may also wish to purchase a crate for the car if you plan to travel your dog in the hatch or with the back seats down. Some crates come with a sloping side that fits hatchback vehicles better than a straight-sided crate. Make sure you measure carefully, and think about where the doors are on the crate. Crates with a door on both the long and short sides can be useful for loading from the hatch and side door, whereas a door on the top of the crate is less useful. If you have a bigger budget, sturdy crates can be custom fitted to your vehicle, which can be worth considering if you don't change your car too often. People who attend dog shows and competitions often favor this option, as the crates can be securely locked, and the vehicle hatch left open for ventilation.

You don't necessarily have to buy a new crate for your GSP if you are buying metal, as a secondhand metal crate is easy to clean and should be durable enough to last. However, do check for any damage, as broken or bent bars may injure your dog. Also, if you are upgrading to a larger crate when your dog grows, you can easily sell a used metal crate in good condition.

Crate training is a four-step process, which may take several weeks or months to work through, but it will be worth it in the long run. You should not simply buy a crate and assume that your GSP will be happy to go in it.

The first step is to reward interaction with the crate. It's important that your GSP can explore it in his own time. Putting treats or toys in the crate will encourage him to go inside. At this stage, you shouldn't close the door, as this might scare him. The aim is simply to make the crate a positive place to be.

The second step is to increase the amount of time that your GSP stays in the crate. You can feed him his dinner in there, or when he goes in, drop treats through the side, so he is encouraged to remain there for a while.

Once your dog is enjoying his interaction with the crate, and is going in and out by his own accord, you can advance to the third step. Start by closing the door for a very short period of time, and gradually increase it. This might just be 30 seconds at first. When you open it again, make sure you reward your dog.

The final step is to leave the room while your dog is in the crate. Again, start with only short periods of time, and gradually work up. Always make sure he has some toys in his crate to keep him entertained while you are not alone. Also remember, he should always have access to fresh water, and should not be left for extended periods of time without the opportunity for a toilet break.

Beds

If your dog will be sleeping at night in his crate, you may think he doesn't need a bed, as you can line it with old comforters, towels or blankets. However, you may wish to put a bed inside your dog's crate, and your dog will also like a bed in another part of the house to be near you during the day.

Choosing a lovely, plush, comfortable bed for your new dog is very tempting. However, if you are about to welcome a puppy, you can be sure your purchase will not be treated with the respect it deserves, and sharp

Photo Courtesy of Taylor Gilliam

puppy teeth will chew it to pieces in no time! What's more, there's a danger the synthetic stuffing used in plush textile beds could be ingested by your curious puppy. So, to start with, a plastic bed is your best bet. It's also easier to clean while your puppy is potty training, and can be lined with old blankets and towels that can be thrown in the washing machine when they become soiled.

Your puppy will also outgrow his bed quite quickly, so you don't want to spend a lot of money on an expensive bed for him at this stage. Buying a bed with lots of growing room may sound sensible, but in fact your dog will feel more secure in a bed that's more suited to his size, so start off with a medium-sized plastic bed, and when your dog has all his adult teeth and has become less destructive, then to treat him to something more luxurious.

Collars, Harnesses and Leashes

The next things you will need for your GSP are a collar, a harness and a leash. Collars and harnesses come with a good range of adjustment, so if you are buying for a puppy, you should look for ones that fit him now on the smallest setting, that you can let out as he grows.

The collar you choose for your dog isn't just a fashion accessory but has two important functions. The first is to carry an ID tag, which is very important with a new dog that may be more prone to run off before he has bonded and received some training. Now is the time to order his ID tag too. You can do this online, or through most pet stores and vets. As a minimum, you should put your cell phone number on the ID tag. Some owners like to include more than one number and a home address. Traditionally, the dog's name goes on an ID tag, but it's said that this can aid dog theft by allowing the perpetrator to call the dog away, so this is a matter of personal choice.

An ID tag is no substitute for a microchip, as the tag, or even the collar, may come off when a dog strays. However, it can mean your dog is swiftly reunited with you if found by a member of the public. This can save possible expenses if your dog has to be boarded while you are traced, or worse still, he's rehomed because tracing you was not possible.

The other role of your dog's collar is to attach a leash for short-leash training. Only a short leash should ever be attached to the collar, as if a dog runs to the end of a longer leash, a sudden jolt around his neck can cause serious injury in this delicate area. It is better to lead your dog from a harness, which spreads the tension across the broader and less vulnerable chest area. In addition, a well-fitting harness is more secure than a collar, which can easily slip off the dog's head if he is wriggling. Harnesses can be made from fabric or leather. A fabric harness will be softer for your puppy, and will usually have a greater range of adjustment, but it's important for your dog's security and comfort that it is well-made.

Choke chains, control collars, halters or control harnesses are not necessary for your dog. You will be training him to walk and respond without these gadgets. Also choke chains, for example, are extremely harsh, and both physically harmful and detrimental to the positive relationship that will underpin your training. Some control halters may be useful with strong dogs; however, you should work on basic leash training before considering this last resort option.

You will need a short leash for training your dog. These are available in leather, chain and fabric. A fabric leash is ideal for your purpose. You might also purchase a long training line for recall training. Narrow webbing or rope is the best material for training lines, especially if you live in a wet country, as wider webbing lines can soak up a lot of water. Recall training is discussed in Chapter 6.

If you're wondering whether to buy a flexi-leash, the use of these retractable leashes is controversial. They do add peace of mind and allow your dog more freedom than being walked on a short leash. However, you should be training your GSP to walk in the countryside with no leash at all, as this energetic breed in particular is better off-leash than on. And when you need your dog to be walking on-leash, for example, near traffic, he needs to be walking closely to heel on a short leash.

Bowls

The only other essentials your dog will need at this stage are food and water bowls. The bowls that your dog uses at home should be heavy to avoid being pushed around the floor. Ceramic is ideal. And when you go out with your GSP, you should take a plastic, metal or silicone-rubber bowl and a bottle of water. Or alternatively, buy a travel drinker, which is a water bottle with a drop-down tray, or any of the similar concepts on the market.

Dog food to go in your GSP's new dog bowl is discussed in Chapter 8.

Toys and Accessories

There are just a few more items remaining that you can pick up at the pet store when shopping for your dog. Welcoming to his new home with a few toys can help to focus his energy, give him something of his own, and divert him from destroying your house on day one. Toys should always be extremely strong for the German Shorthaired Pointer, and anything with a squeaker should be left in the store, as it will only make your dog uncontrollably excitable! A high-quality rope toy is a good place to start, as well as a Kong®, which is a rubber boredom buster you can stuff with something tasty. The Kong® Extreme range is recommended for the GSP.

To satisfy your dog's chewing instinct and help him with teething, you might consider a deer antler, but never rawhide, which is a choking hazard. A Nylabone® is a synthetic alternative that is indestructible.

If your dog is an adult, he might appreciate a Chuckit® ball-slinger, to help you throw an indestructible rubber ball (never a fabric one) a further distance. However, your growing puppy shouldn't be over-exercised, as this can damage his growing joints, so this toy can wait until he is fully grown. It is also worth mentioning that GSPs who will be learning to hunt should not be left alone with balls, which can make them hard-mouthed if they play with them.

A retrieve dummy is another toy ideally suited to your GSP. A rubber ring can also be used for fetch games over short distances while your dog is growing.

A clicker is a particularly useful training aid, and more information is given in Chapter 6.

You might also need some household items to keep your house clean while potty training your puppy. As mentioned previously, carpet shampoo and enzymatic cleaners are important to be able to clean an area which has been soiled, in a manner which removes all the urine. This will prevent your puppy going back to that area to potty again. You may have also heard of puppy pads, which are absorbent pads which you can place inside the house for your puppy to potty on. While these are convenient, they are debatably counterintuitive, as you are teaching your puppy it is okay to potty inside the house. You will find that if you follow the potty training guide in Chapter 6, you should not need puppy pads.

Finally, although your German Shorthaired Pointer doesn't need an array of grooming accessories, nail clippers will be needed on a regular basis unless your dog attends the groomers. More information on grooming is found in Chapter 11.

Introducing Your New German Shorthaired Pointer to Other Dogs

If you already have a dog at home, your new GSP's reaction to it, and vice versa, will depend greatly on whether you are introducing a puppy or an adult dog, whether the new dog has emotional baggage, and the age, temperament and gender of the dog already in the home.

German Shorthaired Pointers have a great affection for humans, but can be mistrustful of new dogs until they get to know them. But they love nothing better than to play, so after the introduction and getting-to-know-you period, they will usually be best buddies with their canine housemates. Where the attraction may be less instantaneous is when you are introducing a livewire puppy with no concept of personal space, to an older dog that just wants a quiet life. Although your senior is likely to give the young upstart a firm lesson in knowing his place, it is very much up to you as the owner to give your resident dog time-out from the attentions of his tiring young new housemate. Crating the puppy when he becomes too much is one way to achieve this. You shouldn't curtail your resident dog's freedom and privileges, as this is unfair and may cause your oldie to resent the newcomer.

Your resident dog may already have had the chance to meet your new German Shorthaired Pointer at the breeder's or the rescue, or even better, on neutral territory. But now you're bringing this newcomer into his territory for the first time. If your dog is used to visits from other dogs belonging to friends and family, he may not initially react strongly to a new dog on his patch, as he doesn't know they are there to stay. But even if your resident dog is a placid character, it's worth taking care with the first introductions, to make sure the relationship gets off on the right track.

Try to get inside the head of your resident dog. He may be confused at being left home alone while the new competitor for his owner's affections is being collected.

You can avoid this scenario by having someone your dog knows well sit with him while you collect your new GSP, and take him out for a walk while you arrive with your new dog. Arriving at an empty house gives your new dog time to explore and find his bearings, as well as anticipate that he will be sharing his new home with another dog by picking up his scent. When your resident dog arrives home, it's best for the first meeting to take place in the yard as long as it is secure, where neither dog feels contained. Be ready for a whole array of emotions, from surprise, to excitement, joy, challenge, resentment and hopefully acceptance. Aggression isn't a natural re-

CHAPTER 5 Preparations for a New Dog

action from a GSP, however, only you know whether your resident dog is capable of it. So, you should be on hand all the while your dogs are getting to know each other, but avoid intervening unless absolutely necessary.

You can also help your resident dog prepare for his new housemate by bringing home an item from the breeder which smells of your new puppy, such as a blanket or a toy.

Be sure to remove any of the resident dog's toys before first introductions, as these could become a focus for guarding. Once the dogs are getting on nicely, a few new toys that neither dog feels ownership over may be introduced.

Your dog might not be the only four-legged resident in your house which needs to be considered. While GSPs and cats do not mix particularly well, it is possible to train your GSP to refrain from chasing them. While you cannot prepare your cats for a puppy introduction as well as you can your dog, providing them with plenty of space to get away from your new GSP will reduce their stress considerably. Cat trees can be a worthwhile investment as they provide your cats with a safe space vertically away from your puppy.

Puppy classes are a great way for your dog to meet other dogs at the same life stage, and are a continuation of the socialization with his littermates that your dog experienced in his first weeks. Your vet will advise you where to find puppy classes in your area. Some puppies may be nervous the first time they attend a puppy class, as lots of lively, vocal pups in an indoor space can seem a bit intimidating. But your dog should soon warm up, especially a curious, fun-loving breed such as the GSP. Try not to fuss over him, and let him join in the fun at his own pace.

Once your puppy's vaccinations are complete, he can also go out and meet other dogs of all ages at the park. This may be his first encounter with adult and senior dogs apart from his mom, unless you have other dogs at home. So, he will need to learn their body language, as it can be quite different from puppy-language. At this stage, there's a good chance he will get it wrong, so it's up to you to keep your dog out of trouble by managing introductions carefully, and always with the permission of the other owner.

Socializing in public spaces should always be on-leash in the early months, and greetings should be kept short and positive, so that your dog doesn't have a bad experience that could set his confidence back. Dogs usually like to meet nose-to-nose, and then may turn and sniff the other end. They should appear relaxed, with a gently wagging tail. If the body and tail stiffen, or the tail starts to vibrate, or if the lips become drawn back, the dog may be ready to snap. This is an immediate signal for you to walk your puppy away, before a positive experience becomes a negative one.

Walking your dog with other dog-owning friends is also a great way for your dog to socialize and get to make some buddies on neutral ground. He can then enjoy play dates with dogs he knows well at your home or theirs, and socialize freely off-leash if the yard is secure.

The main thing to remember with a GSP is not every dog is as friendly as yours, and his boisterous enthusiasm may not be welcomed by senior dogs, less friendly-natured breeds, or dogs that have had previous bad experiences. So, by controlling your dog's encounters, you are giving him the best chance of avoiding confrontation, as well as ensuring your German Shorthaired Pointer is a great ambassador for the breed.

Preparing Children to Meet Your New GSP

It has already been mentioned in this book that the German Shorthaired Pointer is not an ideal breed for you if you have very young children, or plan on having them while your dog is still young. This is because the GSP is so bouncy, and has so little spatial awareness, that he may inadvertently hurt a child that can't get out of his way or that is still unsteady on their feet.

However, if your children are old enough to be taught how to behave around dogs, then the GSP can make a wonderful family dog. Children are full of energy, just like the GSP, so they can form a natural bond, and grow up with the privilege of having a dog as an ever-willing playmate. But before introducing your new GSP to your children, there are some steps you can take to ensure things get off on the right track.

If your children have not had much experience with dogs before, you should take them to meet as many placid and tolerant dogs belonging to your friends as possible, in the weeks leading up to welcoming home your new dog. This is when you can teach your children how to act around dogs.

Explain to your children that they should be very gentle when greeting a dog, approaching him from the side and talking to him softly, and not running straight up to him. Show them how to offer the dog a closed fist to sniff, and then explain where the dog will enjoy being gently stroked – on the back of his neck and his back.

Make sure your children know never to grab a dog's tail, poke his eyes, or fiddle with his ears, and never to try to ride on him, shout around him, or take him by surprise. Tell your children never to pet a dog while he is eating or sleeping.

CHAPTER 5 Preparations for a New Dog

Photo Courtesy of Niki Bobek

As a bouncy breed, the GSP may try to jump up at your children in a way that they probably haven't experienced from the dogs you have taken them to meet. So do tell your children not to get excitable if this happens, and explain that they should always keep their arms down and turn their body away. Jumping up is a behavior you need to train out of your GSP as a priority when you have children around.

Older children can be taught about a dog's body language, and how to spot that when a dog stiffens, draws back his lips or growls, he is not enjoying the attention and may bite. It is also a great idea to involve your children in your dog's daily care, feeding, walking and training, so that the dog learns to respect them, and they learn the responsibility of caring for animals.

When you bring your dog home for the first time, it is massively exciting. But ensure that your children give your dog time to settle during the early weeks. The GSP is a breed that is very easy to wind up, and over-tiring him doesn't mean he will sleep - just as with children, it can mean the opposite! Your dog has a period of adjustment ahead of him, and needs to process his new surroundings, learning what is expected of him, and how to fit into the family. With a little patience, he is sure to complete the family unit, and there will be a lifetime of fun ahead!

CHAPTER 6
Basic Training

Your German Shorthaired Pointer is highly intelligent, and as he was bred to be a working dog, it is in his DNA to be very trainable. The GSP is also a very willing learner, as he loves nothing more than pleasing you and being given a job to do to occupy his busy mind. The key to channeling your GSP's exuberance into obedience is by being consistent and fair right from the start. GSPs respond excellently to positive reinforcement training, but do not do well with harsh correction. You need to embrace your GSP's spirit, rather than break it, when teaching him how to behave. Also, be sensitive to his sense of fun and short attention span by keeping training sessions enjoyable and short. Your dog is smart enough to learn quickly, and needs time to process the lesson of the day. Training should be fun for both of you, strengthening your bond, just as it makes your dog a role model for the breed!

Photo Courtesy of Carly Shotts

CHAPTER 6 Basic Training

Photo Courtesy of Alyson Elwood Autumnglory GSPs

Treat, Toy or Clicker?

Positive reinforcement training is all about rewarding your dog for the behavior you want from him. Punishment forms no part of positive reinforcement training, as it only makes your dog stressed and unwilling to learn. You should set your dog up for success by keeping his targets achievable, and making a big fuss of him when he does the right thing, because the German Shorthaired Pointer loves nothing more than to please the person he adores. Earning your pleasure is a treat in itself for him; however, to motivate him even further, each success your dog achieves may be rewarded with a food treat, a toy or a clicker, or a combination of these.

The GSP is a breed that enjoys food, so in most cases, food treats are an excellent way to train your dog. Bear in mind that training involves many repetitions, so your dog will earn a lot of treats over the session. Therefore, the treats need to be small and tasty, and you should adjust your dog's normal meals accordingly so he is not taking in too many calories. If your dog is happy to be rewarded with his normal kibble, that is a bonus, and you can take it out of his daily ration.

You can buy small training treats from the pet store for convenience, or you can make your own. Your GSP will love tiny pieces of something irresistible such as ham, or a treat that can be stored for longer such as dried liver. There are many variations of the following basic recipe:

Photo Courtesy of Olivia Hutchinson

CHAPTER 6   Basic Training

Dried Liver Recipe

Ingredients:

1lb liver

Method:

1. Preheat oven to 200°F (100°C) and line a cookie sheet with parchment paper or spray with oil.
2. Boil liver for 30 min.
3. Cut liver into tiny, thin pieces.
4. Place the pieces on the cookie sheet and bake for 1-2 hours.
5. Turn the pieces and bake for another 1-2 hours.
6. When completely hard and dry, take the liver pieces out of the oven and allow to cool.

Treats may be stored in the fridge or freezer, or if completely dry, they can be stored at room temperature in a sealed container.

Some dogs may be more motivated by a toy than food treats, especially a playful breed such as the GSP. You will be the best judge of what incentivizes your dog, as long as it doesn't excite him so much he loses focus. When using toys for training, you need to assign high value to the training toy, by keeping it solely for your training sessions rather than letting your dog play with it in his free time. You also need to teach your dog to "drop it" from the get-go, otherwise your training session will become a tug-of-war and your dog will get the upper hand. This can be done with play and reward. Initially, use the command "Drop it" when your dog naturally releases the toy during play, and praise him as if it was intentional, and then ask him to drop it by ceasing play until he drops it for play to be resumed. Alternating two toys can also prompt your dog to drop the one he has.

When using a toy as a training aid, you may require more repetitions of the correct behavior before giving the dog the toy than you would with a food treat, and your sessions may be shorter. You should also allow your dog a longer playtime with the toy to reward him at the end of the session.

GSPs IN LITERATURE
Four Dogs Named Pearl

Robert B. Parker was a renowned author who specialized in the mystery genre. His most popular novels, the Spenser series, follow a detective who owns three German Shorthaired Pointers, all of which are named Pearl. Parker owned a GSP of his own, also named Pearl.

Photo Courtesy of Haley Foster

The clicker is also an excellent reinforcement device. It is easier to use in conjunction with food treats than with a toy, but may be used alongside both. The clicker works particularly well with the GSP, because the breed doesn't concentrate particularly well, but the clicker marks the exact point at which your dog achieved the correct behavior. It is consistent and positive, and helps your dog to focus. If you are looking around for local dog training classes, you should choose one that teaches clicker training if possible. Otherwise, you can reinforce your dog's correct behavior at home during your daily practice sessions with the clicker. Initially, your dog should receive a reward every time he hears a click. Eventually, the click alone is his reward.

Whatever reward you use to train your dog, praise should always follow. Even when you have ceased the food, toy or clicker reward, praise always rewards and motivates your dog throughout his life, as he loves nothing more than to please you.

Potty Training

If you are bringing home a puppy, or sometimes an adult dog that has not been used to living indoors, the first training you will do with your dog is to teach him how to be clean in the house.

When your puppy is very young, he does not yet have full physical control over his bladder and bowels, so you need to be patient and calm, and never punish him for any accidents. You also need to take him outside to potty at frequent intervals so he is not being asked to hold on too long. Set your dog up for success, and he will soon learn the right time and place to potty!

If you have an older dog that has lived outside or in a kennel, he will have the muscle control already, but it may take him a little longer to unlearn ingrained behavior. However, even if he has not lived in a house before, your GSP has a natural instinct not to soil his bed, so if he will tolerate crate training, you still have control over his toileting behavior. But often, older dogs that are not accustomed to a crate may be stressed by confinement. However, the same principles apply – set your dog up for success by taking him outdoors frequently, and praising him effusively for pottying in the right place!

Training your dog to be clean in the house is best achieved by teaching him to potty on command. For this you will need a command word that you don't mind the neighbors overhearing. Popular potty commands are "Busy" or "Potty." Make sure it doesn't sound similar to any other commands you will be using.

As with all the training commands you will be teaching, you should only ever use the word when the dog is actually doing the behavior you are teaching. So, when you take your dog into the yard, he may start running around or sniffing. Watch attentively for the sign he is preparing to potty. Then just as he relieves himself, say "Busy," and make a big fuss of him for being such a clever boy when he has finished. If using a clicker, you can also click and treat to reinforce the point.

You should also use your command word when you take your dog out for a walk. Most dogs will relieve themselves as soon as they start to exercise, and males in particular have an instinct to cover the scent of another dog with their contribution. So, there will be ample opportunity to reinforce your dog's understanding of the potty command. Walking your dog before bedtime is also the quickest guarantee that he will potty before settling down for the night.

Of the numerous occasions when you should take your puppy outside to potty, there are certain times when he is likely to need to relieve himself, so by anticipating them, you are setting your dog up for success. Take him out on waking, after playing, after eating or drinking, when he starts to look distracted, or when he has not relieved himself for two hours, especially if he has eaten.

If you are with your dog when he relieves himself indoors, don't panic or punish him. Simply say "No" in a firm voice, and whisk him outside. If you discover a mess that your dog has made when you were not there, it is too late to react, as your dog will not understand why he is being chastised. Simply clean up the mess thoroughly with an enzymatic cleaner, and resolve to anticipate your dog's needs a bit sooner next time!

If a dog that has previously been clean in the house starts to potty inside again, there may be a medical or psychological reason. If this occurs, you should talk to your vet or behaviorist. Your vet will carry out an examination and possibly blood tests to see if there is a physical cause. If so, medication will usually resolve the problem. Or your behaviorist can help you work out what has upset your dog, and how to help him overcome it.

CHAPTER 6 Basic Training

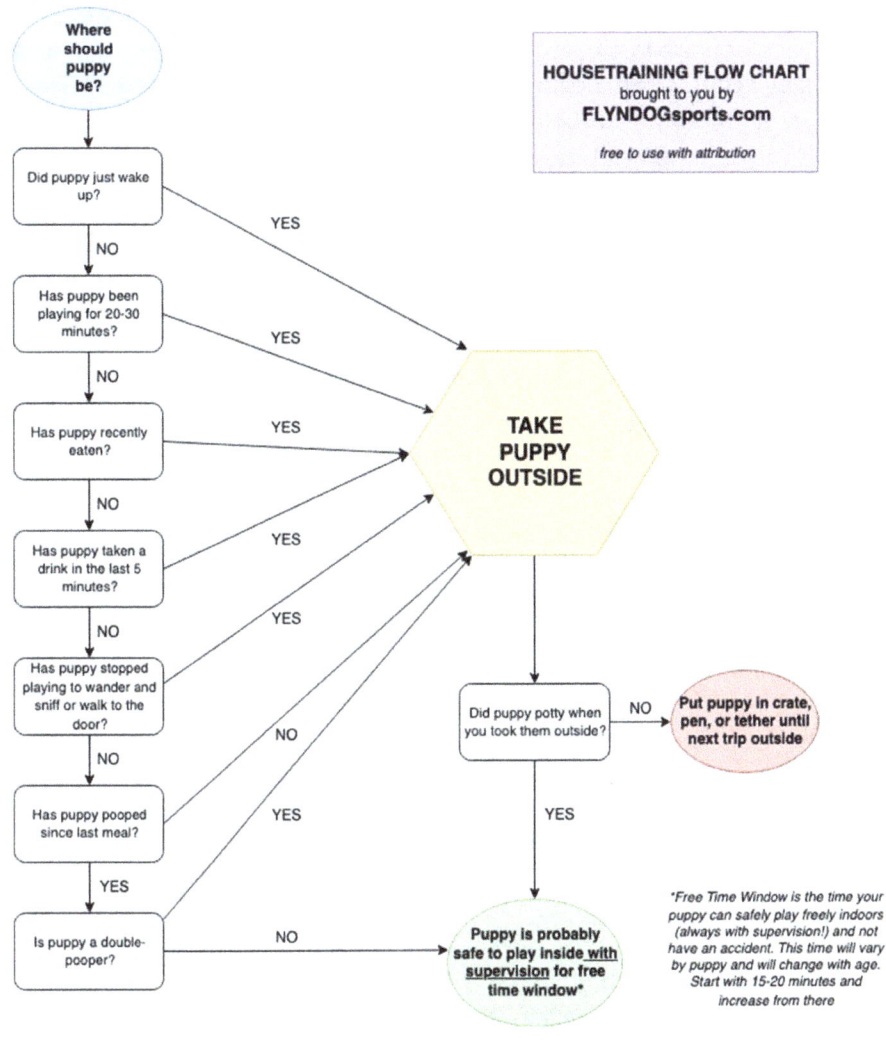

Photo Courtesy
of flyndogsports.com

Obedience Training

If you are attending training classes with your German Shorthaired Pointer, it is important to be consistent with your techniques and to keep practicing the methods being taught in class. For those who are teaching their dog at home, the following methods can be used to teach your GSP basic commands.

Before teaching your GSP any command, you need his full attention. To begin with, you are just going to reward your dog for focusing on you and making eye contact. So, begin by facing your dog. If he is a puppy, you will be more on his level if you kneel. When you have your dog's attention, say "Look at me," and give him his reward. If you are using the clicker, click at the moment he fixes on your gaze, and then treat him. Keep repeating the exercise until he is succeeding consistently. Depending how long you have worked on your dog's attentiveness, he may now need a short break, as it can be mentally exhausting for a GSP to concentrate so long!

Another important command you might wish to teach your dog when you are asking anything of him, is the "Free" command. This gives you control over your dog, so he understands he is not free to do his own thing unless you give him permission.

How to Teach Sit

The next step is to teach the Sit command. With your dog facing you, tell him, "Look at me". Don't click and treat yet as there is more to come! With your treat in your closed hand, bring it to your dog's nose, then up, so he raises his head, and continue the movement over the back of his head. His hind quarters should instinctively lower. As soon as his butt hits the floor, say "Sit," click, treat and praise. Don't say Sit until your dog is actually sitting, as you are teaching him the meaning of the word, not commanding him at this stage. Release him with "Free" before he gets up of his own accord.

If your dog turns or spins as you bring your hand back over his head, you can use your free hand to straighten and guide him into the sit, but avoid using pressure. Just keep repeating until your dog gets it. If this session doesn't go well, go back to the "Look at me" so the dog ends the session on a positive note, and try again later.

With lots of practice and repetition, your dog should get quicker at sitting as soon as your hand goes over his head, and then you are ready to use the word "Sit" as a command, expecting the action for the word alone.

As your dog gets better, instead of kneeling at his level, ask him to sit from a standing position, and then with him by your side instead of facing you.

Sit is an excellent command to give your dog when you need his full attention for the next lesson.

CHAPTER 6   Basic Training

How to Teach Lie Down

Sitting is not the most comfortable position for a dog, so if you are wanting him to stay in one place for any length of time, he should be taught to lie down.

Facing your dog, ask him to sit but don't yet click and treat. Then bring the treat in your closed hand, from his nose, down to the floor, and then draw it towards you. This movement encourages your dog to lower his elbows and creep his paws along the floor in the direction of the treat. In turn this has the effect of lowering the front quarters, and usually the hind quarters will follow. As soon as your dog is in position, use the words "Lie down,", click, treat and praise, and release him with "Free."

If your dog lowers his front quarters but his butt remains stubbornly in the air, don't push him down, but use your free arm like a limbo pole across his back, continuing to draw the treat towards you, so he has to lower his hind quarters under the limbo pole.

Give your dog lots of praise at this low level, so that he doesn't release himself immediately, and you can use the "Free" command to maintain control of the lesson.

"Lie down" is an excellent command for when you want your dog to stay in one place in a relaxed position.

How to Teach Stay

When you have placed your dog in the Sit or Lie Down position, he is then in a position to stay until you release him with the "Free" command. To begin with, you were releasing your dog almost as soon as he achieved the position, so that he didn't release himself on his terms rather than yours.

But now you want your dog to stay in position for more than a few fleeting seconds, so you need to increase the time between your dog taking position, and you releasing him. Your dog will learn that this time period is called "Stay".

To begin with, you may need a helper to hold your dog's collar and gently keep him in position.

Facing your dog, place him in the "Sit". You may then use the word "Stay" as at this point he is staying. An outstretched palm helps to enforce the stay as it puts a body-language barrier between you and your dog. Then step

Photo Courtesy of Gael Sosinsky

back a few paces. Don't ask for too much. If your dog has stayed without trying to move towards you, that's great, however, your helper may have needed to hold him for the first few attempts.

The lesson isn't over yet, as your dog also needs to learn "Come" in conjunction with "Stay". Since you have his reward in your hand he is likely to be very eager to come, so when you are ready, call him to you enthusiastically with his name and "Come". Click, treat, praise and release him with "Free".

Once your helper is not actively restraining your dog while you move away, if the dog gets up, you need to go back and put him back in position, however many times it takes. As he gets better at staying, you can move further away, turn your back on him, and eventually even leave the room! But if he is struggling, go back a step and end on a positive note.

Practice teaching Stay from the Sit and Lie Down positions. If you leave your dog in the Stay for any length of time, he should be placed in the Lie

Down. Remember, an obedient dog will remain in the Stay until he is released, so don't go off and forget about him. If he remains where he is, he may become very stressed, and if he decides to move off, he will set his training back by overruling you!

"Stay" is a really important command if it's imperative for your dog to remain in one place. This might get him out of trouble if you accidentally dropped or spilled something in the house, or your dog is near a potentially dangerous situation.

How to Teach Walk on the Leash

German Shorthaired Pointers are not the best at walking on a leash. They are bouncy dogs and as they grow, they get strong. Nevertheless, there are times your dog will need to walk on a leash, for example out and about near traffic. So, in order for you to walk your dog rather than him walking you, he needs to learn to walk nicely to heel on the leash.

When teaching leash walking, it's important to understand that it is a lesson, and you are not going for a nice walk. This will involve a lot of stopping and starting, and changes of direction, and a lot of focus from your dog. So, he may not tire physically from the lesson, but he will certainly be mentally exhausted at the end!

When you walk your dog on the leash, he should be on your left side, with the leash in your right hand. Make sure you have lots of small treats to trickle feed your dog when he is walking nicely to heel on a loose leash. This is his reward for good behavior. On the other hand, undesirable behavior such as surging ahead, pulling, jumping around or biting the leash will result in you stopping or even walking backwards, effectively preventing your dog from moving forward as he wants to do. Only move forward again when he is settled and the leash is loose. You want your GSP to realize that in order for you both to move forward, he needs to be by your side on a loose leash.

If, on the other hand, your dog plants and refuses to move, don't tug on the leash, but encourage him forward with treats and lots of enthusiasm. He needs to gain in confidence, so praise him effusively when he is walking by your side.

In order for your dog not to anticipate the direction of travel, you should change direction frequently. Keep praising and treating him when he is attentive and doing the right thing. This is a challenge for a GSP, so he needs to feel the warmth of your approval when he gets it right, and will be all the more willing to make pleasing you his life's mission.

Photo Courtesy of Cassidy Flanagan

CHAPTER 6   Basic Training

How to Teach Walk Off the Leash

It has already been said that the GSP is far better off-leash than on. However, until your dog has reliable recall, he can't be trusted to run freely in open spaces. And because he shouldn't be strenuously exerted during his first year while his growth plates are setting, this is the time to put your dog's recall in place, ready for him to enjoy the freedom of off-leash walks as an adult dog.

The obedience training you are doing with your dog in classes or your back yard is already forming the foundation of your dog's recall training. This is because your GSP is learning to respect you, to bond with you, to learn his name and the significance of the "Free" command.

If you have a large yard or access to a securely enclosed field without other distractions, this is ideal to teach recall training. However, if your outdoor space is not enclosed, you could consider using a long training line on your GSP at first, to be sure he doesn't head straight for the hills. You should only attach a training line to a harness and never to a collar, as if he should run to the end of the line, the sudden jolt to his neck could cause serious injury. You should wear gloves when handling a training line, so you can create a bit of tension by running it through your hands before it reaches the end if your dog runs to its fullest extreme.

When you take your dog to the area where you are going to teach him recall, get his attention on you, ask him to sit, and treat him so he knows it is a training session. Then as you unclip the leash, you should send him away on your terms with the "Free" command.

Allow the dog a short time to sniff and play, then at a point where he naturally looks towards you, use your body language, excitement and a treat to lure him back. Only when he is committed to coming in your direction should you use the command "Come," because you do not wish to devalue the command by allowing him to do his own thing while you are calling. In this way, you are setting your dog up for success. Make a huge fuss of him when he has accidentally obeyed you! He will then begin to make a positive association with the command, and come to you through understanding as your training progresses. Never punish your dog by putting him straight on a leash when he comes to you. And if he is being resistant to coming back, don't then punish him with disapproval when he eventually does. Coming back should be full of positive associations!

Keep your dog's focus by changing direction frequently, so he has to keep you in his sights while he is free, and not just assume you are where he last saw you. Also, it may seem counterintuitive, but if your dog runs off, don't run after him, as to him that's a game. Instead, turn in the opposite direction. This is usually enough to catch your dog off-guard, and he will come running back.

When your dog's recall seems reliable, you can take him to secure locations with other distractions, such as the park, to practice coming back in a more challenging environment. You should not practice recall near wildfowl, farm animals or traffic, however, as your dog should always be on a leash in these situations. Also, do not let your dog run up to other dogs uninvited during his off-leash time, especially if they are on-leash.

Toy rewards can be an excellent alternative to food treats when teaching your dog to walk off the leash, as the prospect of a game is attractive to a GSP when he is already excited by being outdoors. But if you are using a ball or fetch toy, this should never be thrown too far or too often while your dog is a puppy.

(In some countries, the e-collar is legal, and some owners choose to use it to teach recall. However, in many countries it is illegal, and can be very harmful if used incorrectly. The e-collar debate is discussed in Chapter 7.)

How to Teach Your German Shorthaired Pointer to be Left on His Own

Separation anxiety can be a real problem for the German Shorthaired Pointer, as he is so reliant on human company. This was never an issue in the evolution of the breed, as the GSP would hunt with his master by day, and come back to the family home overnight. But as the GSP has had to adapt to modern life and becoming a domestic pet, there are occasions when he will need to settle on his own without becoming stressed.

For any breed, there is a universally recommended maximum time of four hours that a dog may be left alone. Whereas some breeds may tolerate being on their own for longer, the GSP is at the other end of the scale, and is not suited to homes that are empty during the day. But it is still possible to teach your GSP to be left on his own, by starting with extremely short periods and working up to a few hours.

If your dog is crate trained, and sees his crate as his safe space, then this is an ideal place to leave him while you are out. As long as he has a bed and some safe toys or an antler to gnaw on, he can relax in his crate and not destroy your home in your absence.

If you prefer to allow your dog more freedom, the room or rooms that he has access to should be clear of any hazards, in case he starts chewing things that are not his. Again, leaving him with an antler and safe toys will give him a diversion. You should never leave your dog unattended with a bone, which may splinter, or a rawhide chew, which is a dangerous choking hazard.

The first time you leave your dog, don't go out of the house. Simply close the door without any fuss, and stay out of sight for a few minutes. If your dog whines, don't return to him until he is silent. Then go back and release him, but again without making any fuss. This first attempt shouldn't be for more than a few minutes.

In contrast to your other training, a lot of praise and attention when teaching your dog to be left alone tells him he was right to be worried, because leaving was a big deal. So, stay calm and unflustered, even if he is being dramatic!

Gradually increase the periods you leave your dog, but be sure to only return when he is quiet. You may find a dog-cam reassuring, so you can check on your dog on your phone while you're gone. That way, you can make sure you are not leaving him alone too long. You might find he is more settled than you realized. Some owners like to leave the radio or TV on while they are out, as it can mask other noises, and feel like human company to your dog.

It goes without saying that if your dog has messed in the home or destroyed anything in your absence, he should not be punished, as this will only increase his stress, and managing separation anxiety is all about keeping your dog's stress levels down.

If you have adopted an older dog, separation anxiety can be an ingrained behavior and harder to overcome than training a puppy. Most rescues will have identified the issue before rehoming, and will only rehome to an adopter that is at home all day and experienced with behavioral issues. But even with an older dog, building up time left alone will help him understand that when you leave, you always come back. If you continue to experience problems, a behaviorist will be able to help you work with your dog. The rescue organization or your vet will be able to put you in touch with a professional, and you should never feel bad about asking for help and advice. You are doing the very best for your German Shorthaired Pointer.

CHAPTER 7
Introduction to Training for Field Work

Photo Courtesy of Samantha Riffle

German Shorthaired Pointers are one of the most versatile breeds for working in the field. They hunt, they point and they retrieve. They are particularly great for gamebird hunting (both waterfowl and upland gamebirds), but they can also scent track wild boar and wounded deer, and dispatch predators such as feral cats and foxes. It's no wonder that the breed dominates the North American Versatile Hunting Dog Association's (NAVHDA) registered dog population.

So, whether you are a professional hunter, looking at exploring it as a hobby, or interested in training your dog in the field to compete in field trials and tests, the German Shorthaired Pointer can fulfill all your needs. This chapter will explore the different options for using a GSP in the field, as well as introduce fieldwork training. However, it will not provide you with all the know-how to train your puppy to become a hunting dog. As mentioned previously, the German Shorthaired Pointer is slow to mature mentally, so this might take up to three years. Also, reading about training is no substitute to getting out and experiencing it, so if you are new to hunting, get in touch with your local club to spend some time shadowing them in the field.

It is worth noting that there are hundreds of different techniques which can be used to train a GSP, and many professional hunters will swear by one particular technique which works for them. Therefore, not all people who have trained GSPs for hunting will have used the techniques in this chapter, and maybe won't even agree with them. Nevertheless, this chapter will provide you with a balanced blend of many popular methods. The GSP is a unique hunting dog though, with a strong character, so just because one technique works for one dog, it won't necessarily work for the next. Therefore do not feel dismayed if you need to explore other training techniques for your GSP.

CHAPTER 7 Introduction to Training for Field Work

Types of Hunting

GSPs are able to hunt, point and retrieve almost all shot animals in the field. These were the original German ideals of the breed and are what the Deutsch Kurzhaar Club of North America now sets as their standards when assessing dogs in field tests.

However, the NAVHDA, hunting clubs and most other German Shorthaired Pointer breed groups have now removed the emphasis on blood tracking, big game tracking and fierceness when dispatching predators, to prioritize the GSP's ability to find, point, track and retrieve gamebirds, such as grouse, pheasants, quail and partridge, as well as retrieve waterfowl, such as ducks or geese, from both land and water scenarios.

Therefore, when researching bloodlines of working stock for your new GSP puppy, it's important not to assume that all working German Shorthaired Pointers are the same in their ability and temperaments. Paying close attention to a dog's registration will provide big clues into his natural fieldwork ability and what sort of work he is best suited for. In addition to this, if you wish to compete with your GSP, or complete field tests with him, not all clubs and associations will have the same expectations for a GSP working in the field.

Photo Courtesy of Micaela Mangum

Choosing a Hunting Puppy

As discussed in Chapter 4, choosing a puppy is not something that should be taken lightly. Researching the breeders and parents is really important, even more so if you buy a puppy destined for hunting.

Many breeding German Shorthaired Pointers are show dogs, selected for their conformation rather than ability in the field. Therefore, they are simply 'gundogs' by name. It is an easy mistake to buy a puppy from a show dog, or worse, an unregistered dog, and then further along the line, find the puppy has no hunting ability at all.

Photo Courtesy of Aaron Retzlaff

CHAPTER 7 Introduction to Training for Field Work

When selecting a puppy for hunting, the main aspect to consider is the working ability of the parents. You might know the parents, and have seen them at work. More likely though, you'll have to research their abilities, which is easily done by looking at their prizes from field trials or tests, or requesting to see whether they have passed a working or natural ability test. The NAVHDA, United Kennel Club (UKC), American Kennel Club (AKC) or Deutsch Kurzhaar Club might be able to recommend highly accomplished dogs from their hunting trials, field tests and meetings. If a breeder says they have hunting dogs, not field trial or test dogs, this is a warning that they don't know much about the breed or they are trying to sell substandard dogs, as field trials and tests are a way of testing hunting dogs. A hunting dog should not be in the field if he cannot pass a field test.

> **WORKING DOGS**
> **TSA Dogs**
>
> The Transportation Security Administration (TSA) employs over 1,000 explosives detection dogs. These dogs make up an important layer of security at airports around the country. German Shorthaired Pointers make up a significant percentage of these canines. Two of these GSPs, Hulk and Orel, were featured in a 2019 publication entitled *Extraordinary Dogs: Stories from Search and Rescue Dogs, Comfort Dogs, and Other Canine Heroes*.

It is important to acknowledge though, that field trial and field test dogs can differ in personality. While they can both be accomplished in the field and be excellent at their jobs, a dog from a field trial line is bred for their extreme drive and huge running nature. Field trial dogs are also typically kennel kept, and are not bred for their soft nature or interaction with people. Not to say some are not great companions, but generally speaking they are not bred for these reasons. Therefore, when purchasing a puppy for working, it is worth establishing whether the parents have been bred for competing in field trials, or as hunting companions and completing field tests, and pick according to your needs for the future.

Some breeders might allow you to go hunting with them to see the parents in action. If you have this opportunity, be on the lookout for dogs which are obedient and have a soft mouth. They should not be stubborn, aggressive, oversensitive, gun-shy or mouth their quarry when retrieving.

Once you've done your homework looking into the parents, you can select a puppy using the methods described in Chapter 4.

*Photo Courtesy
of Dawn Quinn
Gun Dawg Photography*

CHAPTER 7   Introduction to Training for Field Work

Expanding on Basic Training

All working dogs must have basic training as discussed in Chapter 6, as this lays the foundation for all training to come, as well as creates a strong bond with their owner. Hunting training is simply an extension of basic obedience training. Hunting ability and hunting desire cannot be taught. These are a product of choosing a puppy from the best parents. It is a myth that a puppy has to chase game to develop his hunting skills. In fact, a hunting puppy should never chase game, as is mentioned later in this chapter. Your job is to simply channel your GSP's natural abilities into a form which benefits you.

It is preferable to train your own dog, regardless of whether you are experienced or not. It is easy to be tempted to send your dog off to someone professional for training, but this means you will not learn how to understand or work with your own dog. Dogs who are not trained by their owners are far more likely to become confused and have their working ability ruined shortly after coming back to them. However, if you wish to make use of the experience of a professional, if you remain in close contact and get involved with the training too, it will help to achieve the best outcome.

When first starting out, training a puppy with the future plan for hunting is not difficult or time-consuming. All that is needed is plenty of enthusiasm and 20 minutes a day. Most training techniques can be learned from videos and training books; however, your local hunting club is also an excellent resource which should not be overlooked. Most clubs are more than happy to show you the basics, and you can learn a great deal from attending local events.

Training a puppy will vary from dog to dog. Some dogs will be ready to go out in the field in a basic capacity when they are approaching a year old; others may take over three years to become obedient enough and proficient at their task to prevent them from being a liability. Your GSP should take the lead when it comes to progress. Trying to push him to progress quicker than he is mastering things will only hinder your dog. Once the basic training principles in Chapter 6 have been achieved, there are further stages to convert this training into training for work—improving discipline, training retrieving, and introducing a dog to the field.

The E-Collar Debate

Photo Courtesy of Micaela Mangum

If you've ever seen a German Shorthaired Pointer out at work, he may have had an e-collar on (also known as a shock collar or electronic collar). In fact, the GSP is a breed which the e-collar seems to have been specifically made for due to their energy, persistence and ranging behavior. In the US, use of an e-collar in the field seems almost universal. In contrast, the collars are banned in Scotland, Wales, many European countries and parts of Australia. They are also due to be banned in England.

The truth is, e-collars are not required to train a German Shorthaired Pointer, and previous generations have trained their dogs for centuries without electronic devices. Dogs which have not been trained with an e-collar are more likely to perform well in field trials and have more confidence and hunting desire. The use of an e-collar is not allowed in a field trial anyway.

E-collars can be easily abused, especially in young, boisterous dogs who are excited about being out in the field and highly distracted. But if your dog does not have the foundation recall training in place, then an e-collar is not a shortcut to improving that. You should backtrack to improving your dog's obedience before taking him out in the field again. As an example, imagine your dog is running full speed towards a busy main road. You should have the ability to instantly turn your dog around back to you, or ask him to stop his sprint and sit. If you cannot do this, your dog is not ready for the field.

Another reason why e-collars can lead to problems is that if fitted incorrectly, they can lead to an inconsistent contact, and confusing signals or punishment. A collar should be fitted high up on the neck, under the chin for consistent contact, and should not be loose around the base of the neck like conventional collars. The strap should also not be trimmed to length as many straps contain the antenna, and trimming would disrupt the signal from the remote. An incorrectly fitted collar, as is common, can lead to your dog worrying about whether a signal or punishment is coming his way when he makes a mistake.

With that being said, some e-collars have alternative functions which can be helpful in the field. In large open situations, like the plains of Western America, hunters use e-collars with GPS transmitters in them. These are for extreme long-range points, and often result in more ethical kills of the game bird by providing the exact location of the dog on point.

Photo Courtesy of Hunter Herring

Photo Courtesy of Monique Lamke

Some e-collars also have the option of giving off beeps. Signals can be personalized to the individual dog depending on what an owner feels is important. For example, one beep can indicate to a dog to look at his owner, two beeps can indicate for a dog to change direction, and repeated beeps can indicate the dog is being recalled. This is useful, since the ranging distance of a GSP in the field can be far from an owner, out of sight or further than a voice can easily travel. In addition, it is more polite to other hunters, and less disturbing to the game to use a beep signal, than a whistle or shout.

Finally, most e-collars can be used on a vibrate setting, rather than a stimulation (shock) setting, which some hunters use to correct their dogs rather than shouting. While this is more ethical than a shock, it is still a negative punishment, and is a gateway to using the stimulation setting. Scientific research has proven time and time again that positive reinforcement is a much better way to train a dog.

E-collars will always be a topic of debate, and due to their potential to be abused, they are often the focus of many animal-rights organizations. In the end, it is possible to effectively train your GSP without an e-collar, which will result in a stronger bond and more obedient dog. However, e-collars can provide alternative functions other than stimulation, which when used correctly in a positive training manner, can help in long-range shoots.

CHAPTER 7   Introduction to Training for Field Work

Teaching Discipline

Teaching discipline is the first phase in training your GSP to be a working dog. The basic commands will have already laid a foundation for this; however, if your GSP is to make it as a working gundog, he will need more discipline than a family pet. Contrary to popular belief, discipline in a working setting does not need to mean harsh punishments. In fact, positive reinforcement is the most effective method of training a dog, whatever he is being trained to do. Negative punishment will only knock your dog's confidence and impact his bond with you. This is why inappropriately used e-collars can be harmful.

The three most important commands that a GSP must learn are "sit", "come" and "whoa". Other commands such as "hunt" or "seek-up", "fetch", "outside" and "bed" or "kennel" are also very useful, after the first three.

"Sit" will have already been taught in the basic commands stage; however, it can now begin to be merged with "stay" where your dog is required to hold his position until released. You can teach this from the beginning, or you can teach "stay" as a separate command and gradually phase out the stay later on, by always ensuring your dog is sitting when you use the command "stay". Soon he will learn that he should not move from the sitting position until allowed to do so.

"Whoa" is a very important command. This is to tell your dog to "stop moving now". It should not be confused with "sit" and "stay" though. You never want a pointing dog to sit when locating game or when he is on point. Training can be started from a young age by placing your puppy on a table, which requires him to stand still. Even if it is just 10 seconds to start with, this is a good start. It can be gradually increased to a minute, and your dog should receive treats and positive clicks (if using clicker training) when he is still. Moving away from the table, you can then place your dog on a barrel on its side. He will quickly learn that if he moves or even shifts weight, the barrel will become unsteady and roll. This teaches him to remain like a statue when asked to 'whoa.' Once happy with that, the command can be moved to the ground. When your dog is completely still, use the command 'whoa' and reward for remaining still.

You will also have started teaching the command "come", or whatever you choose for recall, during the basic commands stage. But recall in a house setting and recall in the field are two completely different scenarios. Your GSP may have fantastic recall in the house, but might forget the command entirely when there are distractions. This is the point at which most

GSP puppies have an e-collar introduced. But it is unnecessary as long as you have patience and persistence.

It's a common sight for a puppy to run off when distracted and full of exuberance, only to see the owner running after it calling the recall. However, from the very start, you should not let your dog think that running after him is acceptable. When playing with him, allow him to chase you, but you should never chase him. Soon he will begin to learn that coming to you will result in fun, but running away from you just results in him being lonely and the game to end. When taking your GSP out for walks during his early training, try to choose somewhere open, where he can see you at all times, with short grass so that he doesn't accidentally stumble across and flush a bird, which at this excitable stage in life will blow his mind. Walk slowly and allow the dog to run around, but change direction randomly every 30 yards or so, so that he learns to continuously watch you at all times. When he notices you've changed direction and comes running towards you, call the 'come' command and positively reward your dog when he reaches you.

Finally, the command "no" is important in the field for safety reasons, but it must be used with the right timing. A second too late, and your dog will not understand why he is being told no, leading to confusion and a negative impact on your relationship. "No" should always be said in a firm, assertive tone, but you should never shout at your dog or lose your temper.

Teaching Retrieving

Retrieving can be started early on, alongside basic training. At this stage, retrieving should be an exciting game and nothing more. It is not a job, nor is it something that your GSP should get bored of. Keeping up the excitement for retrieving is absolutely essential for an enthusiastic gundog in the future.

You can use any object for your dog to retrieve when he first starts out. This can be a custom-made dummy for training, a teddy, a rope toy; even a ball of socks is suitable. Whatever your GSP puppy finds exciting. Retrieving training should initially be in an area where your puppy cannot get away from you. It is not a game of fetch and chase; your puppy must bring the toy back to you. A narrow hallway in the house is ideal, as then your puppy can only go one way away from you, then either stay away from you or come back to you.

Start by teasing your puppy with the toy, then throw it a short distance. This initially should only be two or three yards. When the dog starts running,

CHAPTER 7   Introduction to Training for Field Work

use the fetch command. Since there's nowhere to go once he has picked up the object, he will most likely bring it back to you, as otherwise he will soon realize that staying down the end of the hallway is very boring and the game is over. When he brings the toy back to you, make a big fuss, and if you are using clicker training, make sure the praise is timed perfectly.

You should never retrieve the toy yourself; that is not your job. If your dog doesn't fetch, gently insist that he does by encouraging him. If he still doesn't pick the toy up, leave it for the day and retry again tomorrow.

The retrieving game should only be repeated three or four times correctly each day, otherwise your puppy runs the risk of losing his enthusiasm for it. Once he is confident at retrieving in a hallway, you can move to a slightly more open area, such as your back yard. However, in a more open area, it is important to have more control over your dog, so always insist that he sits before you throw it, and waits for your command to fetch it. A good amount of time to pause is a slow count to five. This helps your GSP begin to learn that when he is out in the field and flushes something, he must sit and wait for his owner to take the shot before he can fetch.

When progressing to an even larger space, there are likely to be times at first when your GSP becomes distracted and does not immediately return. Remember, as mentioned earlier, this is not a game of fetch and chase, so never go after the dog. Simply turn in another direction and start walking away, giving him the command "come".

Once your GSP has mastered this, you can begin to introduce real birds, but it is absolutely vital that real birds are not introduced too soon. If you are not confident that your dog is entirely in tune with you at all times, delay the introduction of live birds a little longer.

Introduction to the Gun

If your GSP becomes gun-shy, this will ruin his ability to work efficiently as a gundog. An overly sensitive dog will be nervous in the field, and become easily distracted.

Every trainer will have a different technique to introducing a dog to gunfire, and there is no right or wrong way, as long as a positive experience is associated with it. It is useful to have another person helping to ensure that the sound is generated at the perfect time.

You should not immediately jump in with the gun you intend to use for hunting. This is far too loud for your GSP and is likely to scare him. Some GSP owners like to start with loud noises that aren't guns, such as hitting two pots together. Others prefer starting with a low caliber gun, such as blank .22 cartridges or a cap pistol, like what is used on a starting line at sport events. You should not use live ammunition around your dog until well into his training.

The ideal time to introduce gunfire or loud bangs is while your puppy is really enjoying something. For some dogs, retrieving games are incredibly fun. In these instances, the noise should be sounded as your GSP is running towards what he is retrieving. If the blank does not go off, or the person making the sound was not concentrating, never fire the gun too late. Once your dog has reached his toy, he is no longer distracted, and is more likely to notice the gun.

If using retrieving as a learning exercise for gunfire and once your dog is desensitized to the sound, you can begin firing the gun sooner in the retrieve, and eventually, firing while he is sitting before he is given the command to fetch, otherwise he might start thinking that he can run to fetch before the shot has been taken, which is a safety hazard.

However, some hunters like to train their dogs to retrieve as the gun is shot, rather than waiting for a fetch command. Even though this requires a little more trust from your dog and has the potential to go wrong (especially when hunting with other dogs and hunters), it does mean that your dog will get to the game quicker, which is particularly beneficial if the bird is injured and needs to be dispatched quickly to prevent suffering. In the end, it is mainly down to hunter preference.

If you are concerned about damaging your GSP's enthusiasm for retrieving and your dog is highly food oriented, mealtimes are another good opportunity to introduce loud noises.

Whenever practicing desensitizing your dog to gun noises, remember not to overdo it. You don't want your dog to begin to associate food or retrieving with a gun always going off. Three or four times in one session is plenty, and a couple of sessions a week is enough. It does not have to be done every day.

CHAPTER 7 Introduction to Training for Field Work

Introduction to Water

Introducing your GSP to water should be a relatively simple exercise. Most GSPs have a natural enthusiasm to explore water and should not need too much coaxing.

The best place for introducing your GSP to water is a local lake with shallow water at the water's edge. Make sure the water is as warm as possible, and don't let your dog have his first experience on an icy-cold day. A swimming pool is not sufficient, and deep water is also not required. Take the dog up to the water's edge and let him explore, then walk back five yards and throw a dummy or toy just into the water in the same manner you would when you're playing the retrieve game. The water should not be deeper than a couple of inches. Encourage your GSP to 'fetch' the dummy for you, just as you would when practicing land retrieving, and give him plenty of praise when he brings it back. Repeat two or three times, then continue on with your day.

If your puppy is not eager to get in the water, you will need to go in yourself. Even better if you have another dog who loves swimming as he's more likely to follow another dog in to try to continue playing with him. Water is meant to be fun, so give your dog plenty of praise and play in the water when he follows you. If you still have no luck, try again another day. You don't want to knock his confidence. When the dog follows you in consistently, you can start the retrieving game again.

You should absolutely never throw your puppy in the water against his will. This is a sure way to knock his confidence with water retrieving.

Over the following weeks and months, you can start introducing deeper water and swimming, and once confident with the gun, also start firing your .22 blanks when you throw the dummy in the water. Remember, by this stage your GSP should sit when you throw the dummy, otherwise he will get into the habit of fetching before the shot has been taken.

Training in the Field

Like so many dog owners, you probably can't wait to get your GSP puppy out into the field, but this stage should not be rushed. You should have full control over him at all times before you introduce him to large, open spaces. Do not worry if you have to delay it; if you have purchased a puppy from good hunting lines, your puppy will have natural hunting instincts,

CHAPTER 7   Introduction to Training for Field Work

and delaying taking him out in areas with game will not influence his ability to be a good working dog.

Start by letting your puppy run in a large open space with short grass, and minimal game birds, hares or deer. If your GSP flushes something he will probably want to chase it. If he does come across something and disappears, do not punish him when he comes back, as he might start associating game or recall with negativity. As mentioned earlier in this chapter, also do not chase the dog as he runs off. It is easy to try to control this situation by curbing your GSP's ranging instinct, but again, this may hinder his training. Instead, regularly change direction so that he is constantly watching you, and occasionally recall him to make sure he is listening. You can even hide occasionally to encourage your GSP to find you. This not only helps develop his scenting skills, but also, he will find it a great game. The exception to this is if you have started training at a later age, when your dog is likely to be less impressionable and more headstrong. You may need help of a professional if your GSP is consistently running off.

Once your GSP starts ranging further and more independently, and you are confident that you have full control over him, you can start taking him to areas where he might encounter gamebirds. Never allow him to chase or catch anything, and when he flushes something, tell him to sit. If he disobeys, take him home and go back a step to reinforce his basic training. If you allow him to get into the habit of chasing game, he will begin to think that he can hunt for himself, which will prevent him from developing his pointing instinct.

Very little has to be done to develop a GSP's pointing instinct. Time in the field will help him realize that the gamebirds fly away when he gets too close, and very shortly he will start pointing. Some puppies do it from the very beginning with no training at all. Whenever your dog points, always acknowledge him and praise him, regardless of whether he is correctly pointing at game. He needs to start understanding that stopping and pointing is what pleases you, not immediately flushing the game. Only when he is consistently finding and holding gamebirds on point, can you start shooting over him when they are flushed.

Hunting in the field with your dog will be a constant journey of training and improvement, and this chapter just serves as a basic introduction to working your GSP. There are many other techniques to refine your hunting with your GSP, which is why it is important to join your local hunting club or society and participate in field trials and tests. This will help you and your GSP learn further techniques to ensure your hunting experiences are both enjoyable and fruitful.

Ethical Handling of Gundogs

When out hunting with your GSP, do not assume all people like your dog. In fact, some might not like dogs at all and are simply there to shoot birds. To make sure your hunting experience is as enjoyable as possible for everyone, follow these 10 points at all times.

1. Do not let your dog be a nuisance to other people.
2. Do not allow your dog to whine.
3. Do not allow your dog to chase or bite any animal, whether it be other dogs, farm animals or game.
4. Leave the hunt if you are struggling to keep your dog under control.
5. Ask the landowner what is permitted on the hunt and where your dog is allowed.
6. The dog that found the bird has the right to retrieve the bird, even if a different dog's owner shot it.
7. Try not to allow your dog to break at the shot to retrieve another dog's bird. The exception to this is when the bird has not had a clean shot and needs to be retrieved quickly to ensure minimal suffering.
8. Do not hunt with both pointing and flushing dogs, unless your GSP is highly experienced. Their techniques can cause conflict.
9. The hunter closest to the pointing dog has the right to shoot, which is not necessarily always the owner.
10. Occasionally allow inexperienced hunters a chance to shoot over a pointing dog.

Field Trials and Tests

One of the main tests, which all working GSPs should go through, is the Natural Ability (NA) Test, conducted by the NAVHDA. This test can be taken by any dog under 16 months old. There are four phases to the Natural Ability test, and the dog can complete them in any sequence. No game is shot and your dog does not need to retrieve in the NA Test.

- **Field Phase** – Your GSP will be expected to hunt in a field where game birds have been released. He will be evaluated on the use of his nose, searching abilities, pointing, desire to work, cooperation with his owner and gun shyness.

CHAPTER 7   Introduction to Training for Field Work

- **Tracking Phase** – Your GSP will be given the opportunity to follow the trail of a flightless pheasant or chukar. He will be judged on the use of his nose, tracking ability, desire to work and cooperation with his owner.
- **Water Phase** – Your GSP will be expected to swim. He will be judged on his water entry, desire to work and cooperation.
- **Physical Evaluation** – Your GSP will be physically checked over, and special attention will be paid to his teeth, eyes and coat.

After completing an NA Test, your GSP can go on to complete a Utility Preparatory Test (UPT) when he is more trained. Like the NA Test, there are several phases.

- **Field Phase** – Your GSP will be evaluated on his ability to search, point, steadiness on game, retrieving a shot bird and retrieving of dragged game.
- **Water Phase** – Your GSP will be evaluated on his skills to search in water, walking at heel, steadiness and retrieving of a duck.
- **Physical evaluation** – This is the same as the phase in the NA Test.
- Throughout all the phases, use of the nose, working desire, cooperation and obedience are also judged.

After the Utility Preparatory Test, the Utility Test is taken. This is the same as the Utility Preparatory Test; however, your dog will be hunting for at least 30 minutes and his stamina will also be assessed.

Once annually, the NAVHDA Invitational Test is held. The dogs who have performed the highest at the Utility Test will be invited to enter and prove themselves as a truly versatile hunting dog.

The Invitational Test has both a field and water phase where more advanced hunting techniques will be judged, along with cooperation, obedience, desire to work and nose ability. Dogs that pass the Invitational Test will receive the title of 'Versatile Champion.'

The American Kennel Club (AKC) also has tests and events which your GSP can compete in. The AKC Hunt Tests for Pointing Breeds are similar to the NAVHDA's tests. They are pass/fail tests where your GSP is expected to display boldness, desire to work, speed and independence while locating birds from difficult or confusing scent patterns. Judges will look at your dog's ability to find the birds, point and trainability. More advanced tests, known as 'Senior' and 'Master' tests, will also test your dog's ability to retrieve and honor.

Photo Courtesy of Carly Shotts

The AKC also holds field trials. These are similar to field tests but are competitive against other dogs in the same situation. Different pointing breeds will be allowed in the trial, so it will not necessarily mean that you are only competing against German Shorthaired Pointers. The field trials require your dog to display qualities such as intelligence, game finding abilities, courage, and desire to work. Most trials are walking trials; however, some allow the dog's owner to compete on horseback.

The United Kennel Club (UKC) also offers Upland Hunting Program Field Trials for pointing breeds. These field trials more closely resemble field tests as they are non-competitive, and take on similar formats to what is judged in an AKC field test.

However, the UKC does also offer competitions. Along with the United Field Trialers Association (UFTA), they hold a simple competition where style and technique are not what is judged. There is a twenty-minute time limit where your dog has to point and flush, and you shoot three birds. You are

CHAPTER 7 Introduction to Training for Field Work

allowed six shots, but each extra shot will result in a deduction, as well as a partial retrieve, which is judged as when your dog does not bring a bird back to within one step of you. When you bag your third bird and leash your dog, the time is stopped and you receive two points for every minute you have left. The winner is the quickest, with the fewest shots, the best retrieves and the fewest deductions.

The National Bird Dog Circuit and the National Shoot to Retrieve Association also have competitions which allow your GSP to work towards a Champion status, and the North American Deutsch Kurzhaar Club also provides hunting tests to prove your GSP's versatility, so there are plenty of opportunities to get your GSP out in the field in the US!

In the UK, field competitions take a slightly different form. The UK Kennel Club is the overseeing body for field trials and gundog working tests (GWPs – the equivalent of the American field test). Nevertheless, each field trial and GWP is organized by a different field trial society. Field trials and GWTs are nearly always over-subscribed, and priority is given to members of the organizing society, so it is worth joining a few. There are many to choose from.

Your GSP can enter two potential categories; 'Pointers and Setters' or 'Breeds which Hunt, Point and Retrieve' (HPRs). The field trials are mainly held in the autumn and winter shooting season, with the exceptions of Pointer and Setter circuits, being held in April/May and then again in August/September. Field trials aim to bring out the traditional working abilities of the category of gundog which you have entered.

Gundog Working Tests (GWT) on the other hand are designed to encourage a dog's natural working ability and do not involve shooting game. All the work is done with dummies, and they are a friendly way to be introduced to the competition scene. Only the members of the organizing society can enter a GWT. Most dogs won't enter a GWT until they are at least two years old, so they differ from Natural Ability Tests in the USA, which are aimed at younger dogs. There are no GWTs for the Pointer and Setter category though, so if you want to enter a GWT with your German Shorthaired Pointer, you will need to enter an HPR class. Judges will be looking for game finding ability, speed, directness, and control.

***

The German Shorthaired Pointer is considered the ultimate versatile hunting breed. With the correct training and relationship with their owner, GSPs can make incredible hunting companions. So, whether you are new to hunting or a seasoned hunter, a GSP is certain to fulfill all your needs.

CHAPTER 8
Nutrition

Importance of Nutrition

Excellent health starts with good nutrition. By providing your German Shorthaired Pointer with a balanced and nutritious diet, not only will he have all the nutrients he needs to grow, develop muscle and have energy, but his immune system will also be in an excellent state to fight off any infections. So, investing in nutrition will reap its rewards throughout your GSP's life. But nutrition can be a highly confusing topic, and the shelves in the pet food store are packed full of different brands. In this chapter, we'll discuss pet foods, so that you can feel confident in choosing a suitable food for your GSP.

Photo Courtesy of Ellen Kish

Commercial Food

Commercial food is broadly categorized into two types; dry kibble and wet canned food. However, it can be a bit more complicated than this. Food can be dehydrated, raw or cooked, and these processes influence the quality of the food.

Generally, dry food is a better option than wet food for your dog, as dry food provides some abrasion to the teeth as your GSP crunches through it. This in turn helps to clean the teeth. Kibble is also usually more hygienic to handle, and cheaper than wet food in relation to the quality. However, a poor-quality dry food may swell in your dog's stomach, leading to a feeling of bloating and discomfort. So, when you choose a dry food, it must be high-quality.

Nevertheless, wet food can also be a good option for some dogs. It is usually highly palatable, so if your dog is not a keen eater, wet food, or a mixture of wet and dry food, might be the best option for him. Wet food is also good for elderly dogs who have arthritis in their jaw or ground down teeth.

Most commercial foods will be 'balanced' which is a really important aspect when it comes to choosing a food for your dog. A balanced diet will mean a different thing for a puppy compared to an adult German Shorthaired Pointer, and therefore feeding a food which is balanced for the lifestage of your GSP is essential. The American Association of Food Control Officials (AAFCO) sets guidelines for food manufacturing companies, so that they consistently formulate foods which are appropriate for puppies, low-energy adults, high-energy adults or seniors. This is one of the benefits of feeding your dog a commercial food. All commercial foods are regulated, and therefore you can be confident that the meal you are providing for your dog, will enable him to obtain all the nutrients that he needs.

When considering commercial foods, you should look out for the life-stage and breed size specifics. All growing puppies should be given a puppy food. This is much higher in protein, calcium and phosphorus for those growing muscles and bones. Old dogs should be given a senior food. Senior

> **GSPs IN LITERATURE**
> **Colter**
>
> Written by Rick Bass, an American writer and environmental activist, Colter: *The True Story of the Best Dog I Ever Had*, chronicles the best-friend love story of Bass and his GSP, Colter. Colter was the runt of the litter, but almost instantly surprised his owner with his remarkable intelligence and sense of adventure. Rick Bass is a National Book Critics Circle Award finalist and is writer in residence at Montana State University.

recipes have fewer calories, for a more sedentary lifestyle, as well as more omega oils to help with joint and heart health. Your GSP is best suited to a medium or large-breed dog food, as this will contain the optimal amount of protein. You might also notice lifestyle specifics on the packaging, such as 'active.' If your GSP is highly energetic, or you work him in the field, this might be a good consideration to take into account, as 'active' foods contain a higher number of calories per gram, and therefore will help to replenish all the energy your dog is regularly burning off.

Pet Food Labels

Pet food labels can be highly confusing, but it is important to take note of them, as they can tell you a lot about the food.

Firstly, look at the name of the pet food. The AAFCO has some strict rules about how the name can be worded, which gives you a lot of clues about the content.

1. If a product calls itself 'chicken for dogs,' at least 95% of that product must be chicken. The remaining 5% are vitamins and minerals needed for nutritional reasons.

2. If a product calls itself 'beef supper for dogs' or 'lamb entree for dogs,' at least 25% of the named ingredient must make up the product. If there are two ingredients in the name, for example 'salmon and potato dinner,' in combination they need to make up 25%.

3. If the name has the word with, the with ingredient only needs to make up 3% of the product; for example, 'doggie dinner with turkey' is significantly different from 'turkey dinner for dogs.'

4. Finally, if the product says 'beef flavor' the ingredient must be able to be detected, but there are no regulations around what percentage it must comprise.

Next take a look at the guaranteed analysis. This is a table on the back of the packaging which details the percentage of protein, moisture, fat, fiber and ash contained in a dog food. The percentage is based on an 'as-fed' basis, so unfortunately the tables cannot be directly compared between brands. To do this, it needs to be converted into a dry-matter basis. This can be done relatively easily with the help of a calculator. For example:

If you look at a wet food can, it may say that the moisture content is 80%, which means the dry matter content is 20%. If the protein level says it

CHAPTER 8 Nutrition

Photo Courtesy of Danielle Napoli

is 6% on an as fed basis, you can then calculate the protein on a dry matter basis by the simple calculation: 6/0.20 = 30% protein on a dry matter basis.

Equally, if you wanted to compare a dry food to this, where the moisture content was 10% (and therefore the dry content was 90%), and the protein level was 25%, the calculation would be: 25/0.90 = 27.8% protein on a dry matter basis.

So, comparing the two, the wet food has a higher protein content on a dry matter basis. Generally, the higher the protein, the better for your GSP, especially if it's an animal protein, which can be established by looking at the ingredients list.

Ingredients are listed in order of weight. Therefore, if chicken is first on the list, this will be the main ingredient. A quality food should have a meat-based protein as the first ingredient. However, it is worth noting that ground-up dried meat, known as meal, contains 300% more protein than its fresh counterpart per gram, and therefore can be much further down the

list in weight, yet contribute the same, if not more, protein than the ingredient at the top of the list.

There are many potential ingredients in dog food. Meats make up the majority of the protein content, and can be derived from chicken, beef, turkey, lamb, fish, venison and duck. These proteins can be pure meat or meat-derivatives, but the label must state the source. Fish proteins are excellent sources of omega-3 and omega-6, which contribute to healthy joints, skin and coat.

In addition to meat ingredients, there are many different types of grains, vegetables and sometimes fruits. Grains can make some dogs gassy, and anecdotally, can cause skin reactions. Therefore, they may not be suited to all dogs; however, if your dog does not react to grains, they can be excellent sources of dietary fiber to keep your dog regular. Grain-free diets have become somewhat of a craze over the last decade, and in some cases have contributed to the development of heart conditions, such as dilated cardiomyopathy. Therefore, if your dog can tolerate grains, it is better to provide them. Wholegrains are better than processed grains.

Vegetables and fruits are ingredients which contribute most of the minerals and vitamins to a dog's diet. You will most commonly see potatoes, sweet potatoes, peas and carrots listed on the ingredients list. These are all excellent sources of vitamins A, B and C, as well as magnesium, potassium and iron. In combination, this will help keep your GSP's eyes and brain healthy, keep his heart beating in a regular rhythm, boost his immune system, improve the production of red blood cells, and aid in nerve conduction.

CHAPTER 8 Nutrition

Choosing a commercial food can be daunting, and therefore if you are unsure, ask your veterinarian or a nutrition-trained pet shop assistant. They will be more than happy to help you find the most appropriate food for your dog.

BARF and Homemade Diets

Recently, particularly in working dog homes, commercial dog foods have fallen out of favor in replacement for homemade and raw diets. These are also known as BARF diets, which some people say stands for 'biologically appropriate raw food' and others say stands for 'bones and raw food.' Regardless of what it stands for, if you are considering feeding your dog a raw food diet, it is worth acknowledging both the benefits and downsides first.

BARF diets tend to be comprised of uncooked meat, whole or crushed uncooked bones, raw eggs, vegetables and fruit. It is believed to be closer to the diet of the dog's natural ancestor, the wolf. However, it is prudent to acknowledge that the domestic dog is in no way similar to the wolf today. Many people claim when they feed their dogs raw food, they are healthier, have a shinier coat and have a better immune system. However, the diet doesn't come without risks.

Raw food contains numerous dangerous bacteria on them, such as Salmonella, E. coli and Campylobacter. To your GSP, these don't usually pose a threat, as a dog's stomach is used to killing off bacteria. However, to vulnerable people, such as the elderly and young children, infections with these pathogens can be extremely serious. If your GSP eats a raw diet, bacteria can be found everywhere; in the food bowls, around the mouth of your dog, on his coat where he has licked himself, on the surfaces where the food was prepared, and anywhere that your dog has laid his head. Many of these places are easily accessible to a crawling baby.

In addition to the infection risk, BARF foods often contain bones. The argument is that the bones are uncooked, which makes them more flexible and easier to digest in the stomach, however they can pose a risk of blockages and gastrointestinal perforations which can be life-threatening to your GSP.

Finally, home-prepared diets are often unbalanced. This means that the nutrients aren't in the required quantities, which is particularly dangerous for growing dogs. It's not impossible to create a balanced home-prepared meal, however it requires the advice of a veterinary nutritionist, which the majority of people do not invest in.

Photo Courtesy of Flor Bolige Laufer

There are certainly benefits to a home-prepared food, especially since you can locally source the ingredients and even provide organic food if you wish. However, if you want to try home-prepared food with your GSP, it is best to seek the advice of a professional, and adhere to strict hygiene measures to ensure that your dog and family stay safe.

With that being said, there is an alternative. Due to the demand for raw diets, but the high incidence of associated problems, some dog food manufacturers are now producing commercial raw food. The benefit of this is that it has been tested to ensure it is nutritionally balanced and free of bacteria. Commercial raw food usually comes in the form of dehydrated kibble-type food, or frozen raw food, which needs to be defrosted.

Weight Monitoring

Due to the high energy of the GSP, weight monitoring is vital. Your German Shorthaired Pointer can easily burn through his daily calories if he's given enough space to exercise, and therefore ensuring he doesn't become too thin is really important to keep him healthy.

Conversely, as your GSP ages, he is likely to become more sedentary, which will require a very different approach in the food you provide to him. If you continue to feed him with an active or working dog food, he could put on weight very easily, which would put extra stress on his joints and organs.

Each dog is different when it comes to size and weight, which is why it is best to measure any weight changes based on a body condition score. A score of four or five is ideal, and one point up or down corresponds to a body weight change of approximately 5%.

BCS 1 = Emaciated. Ribs, lumbar vertebral projections, and bony prominences around the pelvis are clearly visible. There is severe loss of muscle and no body fat.

BCS 3 = Underweight. Ribs can be felt with ease and might be visible. Not much fat present. The abdomen tucks up at the flank and a waist can be seen from the top. Some bony projections can be seen. Easy to see top of lumbar vertebrae.

BCS 5 = Ideal. Minimal fat over the ribs and can easily feel them. Waist and ribs are visible when standing above the dog. Tucked abdomen when viewed from the side.

BCS 7 = Overweight. Fat present over ribs and need some pressure to feel them. Fat deposits over rump and around tail base. Cannot easily view waist. Abdominal tuck present but slight.

BCS 9 = Obese. Lots of fat around the base of tail, spine and chest. Abdomen may bulge behind the ribs. No waist or abdominal tuck. Fat deposits on neck and limbs.

If your GSP is struggling with his weight being too low or high, the best place to start is by altering how much you feed him. This can be done by looking at the feeding guidelines on the back of the packaging, and feeding him the amount advised for his ideal weight, instead of his current weight. It is best to also take the advice of your veterinarian about what his ideal weight should be, and frequently weigh your dog to make sure his weight is not changing too fast.

***

In the end, since each GSP is an individual, there is not one perfect diet that will suit all German Shorthaired Pointers. Therefore, it is best to seek the help of professionals, such as canine or veterinary nutritionists, veterinary nurses or veterinarians, if you are not sure how to choose a diet for your dog to ensure that he is as healthy as can be.

CHAPTER 9
Traveling

Inevitably, at some point in time, you will need to travel with your German Shorthaired Pointer. It might be on a regular basis, to drive him to your favorite walking spot, or a trip a bit more out of the ordinary, such as a plane ride. The trip might be short, such as a journey to the local vet, or long, such as going away on vacation. Whatever the reason you're traveling and the type of trip you're taking, it's important to be prepared to ensure it goes as smoothly as possible for both you and your dog.

Photo Courtesy of Emilie Becker Big World Photography

CHAPTER 9 Traveling

Preparations for Travel

Preparing your dog for travel starts as a puppy. Not all dogs find traveling relaxing, and ensuring your puppy German Shorthaired Pointer is used to the idea early on will set him up for life. It's likely in these early days you will need to travel with your puppy to the vet several times for the initial course of vaccinations and puppy check-ups, and this can easily sour him on the idea of getting in the car. Therefore, working with your puppy to reassure him that the car is a safe and fun place is important to avoid problems down the road.

You can start by placing your GSP puppy in the car and playing with him for five minutes with his favorite toy. This will promote a positive association. Likewise, occasionally giving your puppy his meal or some treats in the car will also help him connect the vehicle with happy things. Once he seems confident being in the car with the engine off, you can repeat the exercises with the car on. Soon you can progress to short journeys, to the end of the driveway or around the block. After several small trips, you are ready to take your first proper journey.

It's prudent to add that some dogs never like traveling because they suffer with motion sickness. No matter how much you train them to like the car, the sensation of feeling nauseous can put them off forever. This problem can be easily combatted by traveling with your dog on an empty stomach (or relatively empty in the case of a puppy, as puppies shouldn't ever be starved), or requesting a prescription for anti-nausea medication from your veterinarian to preempt the travel sickness.

Once your German Shorthaired Pointer is mentally ready to travel, you must also prepare for your trip. Regardless of where you are going, you should always prepare some essentials for your GSP. A bowl and bottle of fresh water is vital, as even if you are not traveling far, there is always the possibility of your car breaking down or traffic jams, and you being out longer than expected. A dog should never be without access to fresh water.

If you are traveling to a far location, for example on vacation or to a field trial, checking in with your veterinarian before your trip is a wise idea. This will give him the opportunity to check your dog over and ensure he doesn't have any health concerns that should be addressed prior to your trip. It also gives you the opportunity to check that your beloved dog's microchip is working in case he gets lost while you're away, and allows you to pick up any chronic medication or flea and worming treatment. If you're flying, you might need to check that your dog's vaccinations are up to date, especially rabies, and make sure your vet has filled out your pup's passport and certificate of health, depending on the destination you're traveling to and what the requirements are.

Ensure that you have your vet's number pre-programmed into your phone, so that if your GSP has to visit a vet while you are out of town, you can quickly provide the details of your regular vet so that the veterinarians can exchange medical histories, if relevant. It is also useful to do your research, and investigate which is the closest veterinary practice to where you are staying. Pre-program this number into your cell too, so you will not waste time searching for a local vet practice in an emergency.

Photo Courtesy of Kelsey Knapp

CHAPTER 9 Traveling

Photo Courtesy of Mike Harris

Traveling in a Car

Where you choose to let your German Shorthaired Pointer sit in the car is ultimately your choice; however, there are several different options to suit you. If you have a particularly large car, a crate in the hatch or on the back seat might suit you best, as this provides a safe, confined space for your GSP. A crate should be made of sturdy material which is easy to clean, and be placed in the car where there is adequate ventilation. Your GSP should be able to easily stand, sit, lie down and turn around in the crate without discomfort.

Another option, which many people choose, especially if they are in the countryside often, is traveling your dog in the hatch of the car. This gives him space to move around and ensures that only one section of your car gets dirty. A guard between the hatch and the back seats will prevent your dog from thinking he can join you in the front, and keep you and your passengers safe. The downside to traveling in the hatch is that if you have a car crash, your dog could potentially be injured, as he will not be fully restrained. Some cars have a place in the hatch where you can attach a car harness, which is a good compromise. However, you should be aware that the hatch is a crumple zone in the event of a rear end collision.

A car harness, however, is used more frequently if you choose to sit your GSP in the back seat of the car, as most car harnesses attach to the seatbelt or seatbelt clip. Since the German Shorthaired Pointer is a larger breed, your dog won't leave much room for any passengers on these seats, so this option is only viable if you're traveling alone or only with one other passenger. If you have been out for a walk in the country, or out working your dog on the hunt, chances are your GSP won't be particularly clean when he gets back to the car. But this shouldn't be a concern, as dog carseat covers and hammocks are available for most types of car, which protects your car from mud and hair.

Anywhere you go, make sure you take a leash, water and food. You should offer your dog food at least every 12 hours, and water at least every 4 hours. Your dog should also be given ample opportunity to relieve himself and burn off some energy. If you need to stop to fill up with fuel, remember, dogs die in hot cars very easily. This can be prevented by ensuring a window is open, you are parked in the shade, and there is plenty of fresh airflow to where your dog is sitting.

Traveling by Plane

If you are traveling with your dog via plane, you should ensure you are well prepared. Every airline has different requirements for traveling with dogs, and therefore even if you and your dog have plenty of air miles to your names, you shouldn't assume you know all the requirements every time. Therefore, each time you travel, be sure to check for any new requirements from an airline. If you show up unprepared, your dog may be denied the right to travel.

Since the GSP is a medium to large breed, your dog is likely to need to travel in the hold. The exceptions to this are if you have a small, young GSP who can fit at your feet, or if your GSP aids you as a therapy dog. All airlines will require your dog to travel in an airline approved crate in the hold. The details of what they deem suitable will be on their website. Most airlines also require you to present a certificate of health from your veterinarian to prove that your dog is fit to fly. This is usually in addition to a passport, vaccination history and export paperwork, depending on your destination. Your veterinarian will be able to advise you on what you need.

CHAPTER 9 Traveling

You won't be able to fly your GSP if he is under 12 weeks old, or the temperatures on departure, arrival and connections are below 45 degrees Fahrenheit or above 85 degrees Fahrenheit, so it is important to check the forecast before booking your tickets.

If it is your first time flying with a dog, employing the aid of a pet travel agent will help relieve the stress of the journey, as they will organize all the details and paperwork on your behalf. That way you can be sure that everything is in place.

Photo Courtesy of Emil Mansour

Photo Courtesy of Jake and Nicolette Arnitz

CHAPTER 9 Traveling

Vacation Lodging

When booking your vacation lodging, not all places are dog friendly. In fact, even those which are dog friendly may only accept small dogs, so it is worth phoning the hosts or establishment to check that it is all right for your GSP to join you.

QUOTE

"Breed a Boxer with a German Shorthaired Pointer, you get a Boxershorts. A dog never seen in public"

Good Dog! magazine

When you arrive, it is important to be courteous and remember that even though it is a pet friendly place, not all guests will necessarily like dogs, so try to keep your German Shorthaired Pointer relatively inconspicuous, which may not necessarily be easy with his boundless energy! Ask where you can walk your dog and where he can potty, and be sure to always clean up after him.

Try to stop your dog from barking by not leaving him alone in this strange place. This will also prevent him from chewing furniture if he is naturally anxious. If he is crate-trained and you have brought his crate, your dog will have the advantage of a familiar, safe place where he will feel more at home, and you can relax knowing he is not causing any damage.

Likewise, try not to let your GSP damage anything within the lodging, and be sure to clean before you leave, as your accommodations should not require a deep clean by the staff before the next guest arrives.

Leaving Your German Shorthaired Pointer at Home

If you cannot take your German Shorthaired Pointer with you on your trip, there are several options for keeping him at home. Not all options are suitable for all dogs, and therefore choosing the one to best suit your needs and your GSP's personality is vital.

The first option is to board your GSP with a reputable boarding kennel establishment. The benefit of this is that boarding kennel staff are highly experienced with dogs of all different personalities and therefore you can rest assured that your GSP is being well cared for. However, at a boarding kennel, most dogs remain in their allotted space for the majority of the day,

Photo Courtesy of Rhonda Zimmer

only being allowed out into a run or taken for exercise once or twice a day. Since the German Shorthaired Pointer is an energetic breed, this might not suit all GSPs and you may come back to your GSP climbing the walls with explosive energy! If you do choose to place your GSP in a boarding kennel establishment, be sure to drop in unannounced to look around before booking his place. This will ensure that you truly see what the conditions are like and whether the dogs seem happy. Finding a reputable kennel is really important for the safety of your dog, and therefore don't be shy to ask about the staff's qualifications, as well as research previous client reviews.

The second option is to take your German Shorthaired Pointer to a friend, family member or his breeder. This ensures your dog gets plenty of one-on-one attention and love. He is also more likely to get a suitable amount of exercise in this setting. If the person who has agreed to look after your GSP has another dog, first check that the two animals get along before finalizing arrangements. A meet and greet in a neutral territory is the best way to introduce them, as then your dog is not invading another dog's personal space. Reciprocal arrangements can work very well with dog-owning friends or family members, so you can look after each other's dogs whenever either of you travel. For the dogs, this is also a good arrangement as they become familiar with the carer, their dog and their home.

The final option is to hire a pet sitter. These are professionals who come and stay in your house when you are away. Occasionally, pet sitters come in daily to walk your dog and then leave later in the day. Therefore, be clear about which one you wish to hire when making reservations with the pet sitter. The benefit of them staying at your house is that you know your house is being looked after, and your dog gets to remain in familiar territory. If you decide this is the best option for your dog, be sure to allow several meetings between your dog and the sitter before they come to stay, to ensure your GSP is happy and comfortable around them. Apart from hiring a professional, you may be fortunate to have a family member or friend who would be happy to live in your own home while you are away, and care for your dog.

Only you will know what is best for your German Shorthaired Pointer; whether to travel with him or leave him behind. But whatever you choose to do, holidays should be enjoyed by all, so take time to plan it well and then you will be able to enjoy your travels to the fullest extent.

CHAPTER 10
Dental Care

It goes without saying that brushing our teeth is part of a normal daily routine, and therefore it is surprising that many dog owners do not consider it necessary for their dogs. A common reason is because owners believe that since dogs in the wild do not need their teeth brushed then neither do their domestic counterparts. But this is far from the truth. The diet of domestic canines is very different to that in the wild, and as a result, the dental health of domestic dogs can be rather poor if not addressed early on. Your GSP also has a longer life expectancy than his wild ancestors, so his teeth need to last him into his senior years. If you want your German Shorthaired Pointer to have a comfortable mouth and fresh breath, teaching him about dental care from a puppy will make both of your lives much easier.

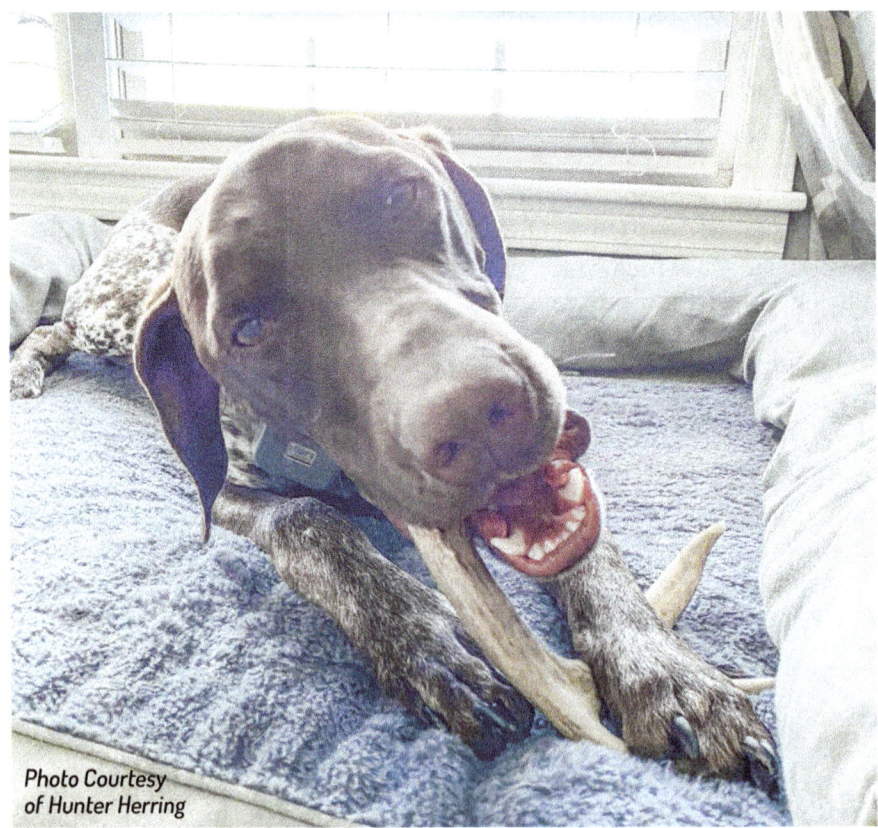

Photo Courtesy of Hunter Herring

Importance of Dental Care

Oral hygiene is closely linked to internal health, and if your dog has a mouth full of tartar and bacteria, he will not only be uncomfortable, but his nutrition will also suffer and he will be constantly swallowing harmful bacteria.

If allowed to get to this point, the only way to correct the mouth is with a dental procedure, which can be costly and require a general anesthetic. But with daily oral care, this can be avoided.

> **WORKING DOGS**
> **Haus**
>
> In 1942, the United States Air Force Air Combat Command established the 380th Air Expeditionary Wing. The provisional unit is comprised of around 1,200 members, including a German Shorthaired Pointer named "Haus." Haus has been trained to sniff out explosives and is tasked with searching vehicles and packages for explosives before they enter the base.

Dental Anatomy

A tooth is a bony structure made up of a crown above the gums, and a root or roots below the gums. There are 28 deciduous (puppy) teeth which appear within the first few months of life. These fall out, and are replaced by 42 adult teeth between the ages of four and eight months. This is why puppies tend to chew on everything, because the process of teething can be itchy and uncomfortable.

The small teeth at the front of the mouth are called incisors. These would have been used by dogs' wild ancestors to nibble meat off the bone. Next to them are the long canines, used for grabbing hold of prey in the wild. Inside the cheeks are bigger flatter teeth called the premolars and molars. These are used to grind harder food.

Even though the teeth are mainly made up of bone, there are other elements to them as well. The outer layer of the tooth is enamel, which is a protective layer. Inside the middle of the tooth is the pulp, which is a fleshy section made up of nerves and blood vessels. This supplies the tooth with all the nutrients needed to survive, and if it becomes exposed, it can cause considerable pain. Around the root of the tooth is the tooth socket. This is a dip in the jaw where the tooth sits. Holding the tooth in the socket is a tough structure called the periodontal ligament. When there is dental disease, this ligament weakens, leading to the tooth becoming wobbly and eventually falling out.

German Shorthaired Pointers have lovely long noses, so it is easy to pull their cheeks back and examine the entirety of their mouth, unlike brachycephalic (short-nosed) dog breeds such as Pugs.

Tartar Build-Up and Gingivitis

Tartar is a build-up of leftover food and bacteria around the base of the tooth, where the junction of the crown meets the root and the gumline. It's really important that tartar isn't allowed to build up, as the body tries to combat the bacteria by sending inflammatory white blood cells to the area. The closest these inflammatory cells can reach is in the gums, and since this does not kill off the bacteria in the tartar, it results in the gums becoming more and more sore; a syndrome known as gingivitis. Gingivitis is extremely painful and can have serious consequences. As the gums swell, the periodontal ligament which holds the tooth in the socket becomes weakened, and eventually the tooth starts to wobble and fall out. This is not always a fast process, and teeth can remain wobbly for months or years, which can be painful for your GSP.

Preventing tartar build-up will help prevent gingivitis, which can be achieved through diligent dental care and brushing. If it has become severe, or the tartar has become mineralized (known as calculus), it is impossible to remove it without a dental procedure, which is discussed later in the chapter.

Dental Care

Dental care should be part of every dog owner's routine, and once it becomes a habit, it should take no time at all. Dental care starts by simply examining the mouth. Fully checking every aspect of the mouth should be done every few weeks, and then you will notice any changes quickly. If your GSP is a working dog, he is probably more at risk of sustaining trauma to his teeth than a household pet, and therefore this is even more important for him. To check the mouth, first start with the incisors, then work backwards to the molars by pulling the cheeks right back. Check all aspects of the teeth; the cheek side, tongue side and the chewing side, for any tartar build up, trauma or discoloration.

CHAPTER 10   Dental Care

The next step to routine dental care, which provides the mainstay of treatment, is brushing your dog's teeth. This should start when your dog is a puppy. If you only start once there is dental disease, it is impossible to undo the damage already done. Brushing teeth is not something many dogs will tolerate if only introduced at an older age, and therefore teaching your GSP puppy that dental care is a fun and positive experience from a young age will reap its rewards later in life. You can do this by gradually introducing the concept of brushing by placing a small amount of toothpaste on your finger and inserting it into the mouth, then praising with treats and attention. The next day, progress to a small amount of brushing on a toothbrush, and similarly, greatly reward your puppy afterwards. This can gradually be built up to a full brushing session, but remember never to forget the praise afterwards.

Photo Courtesy of Melissa Moore

Brushing should be done with dog toothpaste only. This comes in a variety of flavors which are palatable to dogs, and contains enzymes that help to dissolve the tartar. You should never use a human toothpaste, as it can be toxic to dogs. Since German Shorthaired Pointers are large dogs, using a human toothbrush with firm bristles is fine, however you may find a dog toothbrush easier to use, as these toothbrushes have angled heads to make it easier to reach the teeth at the back. Start by brushing the front teeth, then pull the cheeks far back to brush the molars. If your dog will let you, slightly open his mouth to also brush on the tongue aspect of the teeth. A brushing session should last at least a minute, but quality and a positive experience is more important over quantity. When you are done with brushing, don't forget give your dog plenty of fuss and rewards.

Dental brushing can be complemented with the use of dental chews. They are not a replacement for brushing, but can be useful to make sure the

Photo Courtesy of Mike & Lindsay White

teeth are clean in between times. The concept behind dental chews is that they are shaped so that they cause friction, abrasion or suction to the tooth, so that tartar which has not yet become too adhered comes off. Don't forget treats contain calories though, so remember to alter how much you feed your dog if you are also giving treats.

In a similar manner to how dental chews work, dry kibble also provides friction on the teeth which helps to keep them clean. The larger the kibble the better, and some pet food manufacturers make 'dental food' that has specially shaped kibble for this purpose alone.

Finally, another option is to use dog dental wash. Like toothpaste, you should never use human dental wash as this can be toxic to your dog. Dental wash is not a replacement for brushing, but it usually contains the same enzymes which are in the toothpaste, so as it hits your dog's teeth, it helps to dissolve some of the tartar. If there is extensive tartar build-up, it won't solve the problem, however it can prevent it from getting worse. Dental wash is easy to use. Some products are sprayed into the mouth, directly on the teeth, and other products need to be added to fresh drinking water every day.

Dental Procedures

If your dog has advanced dental disease and teeth which need to be extracted, or a large build-up of tartar which cannot be addressed by brushing alone, he may need a dental procedure. Dental procedures aim to create a healthy oral environment, by removing tartar, calculus, bacteria and wobbly teeth.

A dental procedure requires a general anesthetic; however, your GSP will only need to be at the vet clinic for the day, and will be ready to go home in the afternoon once he's woken up. The procedure will start by scaling off all the tartar from the teeth to decrease the bacterial burden in the mouth. After that, the vet will probe around every tooth to investigate whether any need to be removed. If they do, he will loosen the periodontal ligament with a special tool called an elevator to be able to extract the tooth. If the socket is large, your vet might choose to suture it closed to prevent food from packing into it. After this, your dog's remaining teeth will be polished, and his mouth will be rinsed out.

After a dental procedure, your GSP will probably be sent home with pain relief and antibiotics if he has had tooth extractions. He may feel off color for the rest of the day, but most dogs are back to normal the following day. In addition to this, your dog's teeth will be pearly white like they were when he was a puppy!

Even though it might seem invasive to book your dog in for a dental procedure, he will feel so much better afterwards, with a pain free mouth, and you will enjoy having a German Shorthaired Pointer with fresh breath!

CHAPTER 11
Grooming

The upkeep of a German Shorthaired Pointer's coat is rather simple. The GSP is not a breed which needs a trip to the groomer's every month, and when coming home from a walk out in the countryside or a day out hunting, cleaning simply requires a quick shower or hose down, and not endless untangling of undergrowth and burrs. Nevertheless, grooming extends further than coat upkeep, and nails, ears and anal glands also need to be considered. This chapter details different aspects of grooming which will need to become routine for your German Shorthaired Pointer to remain in top health.

About the Coat

The German Shorthaired Pointer has a relatively easy coat to maintain. The coat is short and smooth, which means trimming or shaving the hair does not form part of the grooming routine. It is double-layered, which means it has a fluffier undercoat to keep warm and a coarse topcoat which acts as a waterproof layer.

German Shorthaired Pointers mildly shed year-round, with a heavier shedding season twice yearly in the spring and the fall. Routine coat brushing will reduce the dead hair from shedding in your house, which will keep your house much cleaner, as short hairs can become embedded in soft furnishings where they are difficult to remove.

> **GSPs IN LITERATURE**
> **Run, Rainey, Run**
>
> Mel Ellis was a Wisconsin journalist who wrote for several periodicals, as well as published 18 books, three of which were adapted into Disney films. His 1967 book, Run, Rainey, Run, tells the story of Ellis' own dog, Rainey, a German Shorthaired Pointer, and their adventures hunting and living together.

Coat Health

Brushing the coat of a German Shorthaired Pointer is relatively simple. The best brush is either a brush with firm bristles or a rubber grooming mitt. Wire brushes and combs are unnecessary. Simply brush in the direction of the coat all over, and that's it! There is no need to wet the coat or part the hair, like other breeds, as the GSP has a very easy coat to manage. To prevent hair fall, brushing the coat three or four times a week will pick up loose hairs.

Occasionally your GSP might need a bath, but bathing him too frequently will remove the natural oils in the coat which damages the health of the hair and skin, as well as removes its natural ability to stay water resistant. Bathing should only happen when absolutely necessary, for example if your GSP becomes dirty or smelly. This might be fairly frequent if your GSP suffers from Malassezia dermatitis, as discussed in Chapter 13. But if your dog has no underlying health issues with his coat, a bath once a month or even less frequently is ideal.

When you bathe your GSP, you can place him in the bathtub or in an outdoor children's paddling pool, and either use a showerhead or hose, depending on how warm the weather is. Start by wetting the coat, and then apply a mild canine shampoo as human shampoo can irritate. Lather the shampoo all over your dog's back, neck, chest, belly and legs, then clean his head with a washcloth, ensuring shampoo does not get in his eyes. Afterwards, rinse completely and towel-dry.

If your GSP comes back home after being out, and is covered in mud, he can be rinsed off more frequently than this, but shampooing should not be a frequent occurrence.

Photo Courtesy of Elik Taschner

Nail Clipping

Keeping your dog's nails short is important for his health, as when the nails are allowed to get too long, they can curl around into the pads, causing extreme pain. Older, arthritic dogs also struggle to walk with longer nails. In addition to this, your dog is more likely to sustain nail trauma when out in the countryside if his nails are long in length.

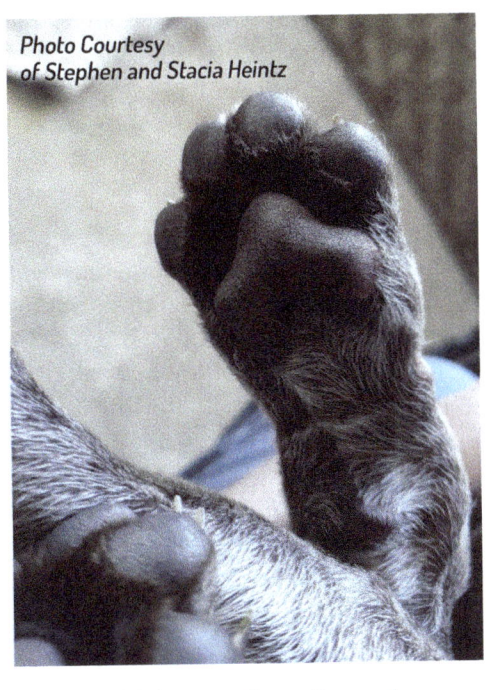

Photo Courtesy of Stephen and Stacia Heintz

You can clip your dog's nails yourself. However if you are not confident with the technique, a groomer, vet or vet nurse can help you. Nails should be checked, and clipped if necessary, every month, but the need may decrease if you walk your GSP on hard surfaces frequently as these surfaces act as natural abrasives which wear down the nails.

The nail has a fleshy center to it called the quick. This contains nerves and blood vessels and should be avoided when clipping the nails. If your GSP has clear nails, it will be fairly easy to see, however if he has black nails, it may be a bit of a guessing game. Sometimes, if you turn the paw upside down, you can see the quick in black nails from the bottom, but this is not always the case.

Gradually cut the nail shorter, a little at a time, using a dog large nail clipper. The cut should be parallel to the ground. If you are nervous about cutting the quick, nail grinders are also available on the market, which slowly grind down the nail, making it less likely for you to catch the quick.

If the nail does bleed, try not to panic, otherwise your dog may also panic. Simply apply pressure to the nail for five minutes using a wad of cotton wool. Alternatively, you can purchase a silver nitrate pen, which is an excellent cautery device and very easy to use. All that is required is to dab the area with the pen, and the bleeding stops within seconds.

Ear Cleaning

Ear cleaning is a vital part of grooming, especially if your dog spends a lot of time in the countryside. Ear cleaning helps maintain the ear canal at a certain pH which prevents bacteria from proliferating, resulting in fewer ear infections. There are many ear cleaners available to purchase, but the most reputable are available from your veterinarian. Ear cleaning should be done weekly or after every swim.

The inside of the ear is made up of several sections. The first section of the external ear canal is called the vertical canal, which travels down towards the ground and then turns 90 degrees and travels into the head towards the brain. This section is called the horizontal canal. It is met by the tympanic membrane at the end, which is a very small sheet of tissue. If this becomes ruptured, then infections can travel deeper into the ear and become serious. After the tympanic membrane is the middle ear, followed by the inner ear. Infections in these regions can affect balance and are extremely painful, whereas infections in just the outer ear will be very itchy and cause scratching and shaking of the head.

To clean your dog's ear, all you need to do is lift up the pinna (the ear flap), place the nozzle of the ear cleaner as deep into the vertical ear canal as you can, and give a squeeze. Quickly place the pinna of the ear over the exit to the canal so that no ear cleaner can come out, and massage the area

for about 30 seconds. This allows the ear cleaner to do its work and loosen the wax. When you let go, take a step back, as your dog will want to shake his head. This is a good thing as it gets out all the ear cleaner and wax, but it can be messy and you don't want to be in the firing line! Once your dog has finished shaking his head, take some cotton wool and wipe clean everything that has come out.

Anal Glands

The anal glands are two anatomical sac-like structures that sit just inside the anus. They are redundant and have no physiological purpose, however occasionally they can cause problems as they can easily fill up with fecal material. If left unexpressed, this can lead to anal gland infections and abscesses, which can be painful and detrimental to your GSP's health.

Expressing anal glands is not a pleasant task, and even though it is a technique which is relatively easy to learn, most owners choose to get their groomer, vet or vet nurse to do it for them. When they are full, they are likely to give off a pungent fishy odor and your dog will scoot his bottom along the ground. Expressing the glands, or at least checking them, should be done once every few months even if there aren't any problems, and not only when your dog is scooting.

To empty them, the anal glands need to be squeezed with one finger on the inside and one finger on the outside of the anus. They are in the 4 o'clock and 8 o'clock positions and usually relatively easy to feel. Once the material in them is expressed into a tissue, your dog will immediately feel better. If the glands need to be expressed frequently though, further treatment may be required, such as firming the stools with supplements, or removing the anal glands surgically.

*****

Keeping your German Shorthaired Pointer well-groomed is not too challenging compared to long coated breeds of dogs, but nevertheless it shouldn't be neglected. Your GSP will thrive on the extra attention, and not only will it improve his health, but it will improve your bond too.

CHAPTER 12
Preventative Health Care

The best way to ensure your German Shorthaired Pointer stays in top health is to prevent health conditions, rather than react to them. This is why preventative health care is vital. Your veterinarian can help with this. After all, since the GSP is prone to many genetic health conditions, as discussed in Chapter 13, having a vet on board will help you keep your GSP in tip-top condition.

Photo Courtesy of Flor Bolige Laufer

CHAPTER 12   Preventative Health Care

Choosing a Veterinarian

There are many benefits to always seeing the same veterinarian. Not only do they know you and your German Shorthaired Pointer, and become familiar with your dog's common ailments, but also your dog becomes familiar with them, which helps to ease the anxiety which usually accompanies a trip to the vet.

So, to ensure you find a veterinarian who you can remain with for the lifetime of your dog, you will want to consider many aspects which might be important to you.

Qualifications

All veterinarians have to be qualified from vet school and have passed the board exam in the state they work in; however, some veterinarians have further qualifications too. This might be important to you if you are particularly concerned about a certain aspect of your GSP's health.

Having access to veterinarians in your local veterinary clinic who specialize in subjects such as dermatology, ophthalmology or orthopedic surgery may prevent the need for a trip to a referral hospital if your dog becomes ill with something a little unusual. This can be a real bonus as not only does it prevent you from having to travel to an unfamiliar veterinary hospital, which may not be local to you, but it is usually also easier on your finances.

After-Hours Emergencies

There are two ways in which vets usually handle after-hours emergencies; in-house or referral. Some veterinarians like to offer after-hours emergency services to their clients to give them the option to take their pet to a familiar place. This is nice, as it ensures you see a familiar face, and your GSP will stay in one place if hospitalized for any length of time.

Other vets employ the services of an after-hours emergency specialist. These are central veterinary practices that only work in the evenings, nights, weekends and holidays. The benefit of this is that the vets working in these environments

CELEBRITY DOGS
Copper Hunt

American country music singer Sam Hunt adopted a brand-new German Shorthaired Pointer puppy named Copper in 2020. Hunt adopted the puppy around the same time that his album, Southside, was released.

Photo Courtesy of Ashleigh Scialo

are more experienced with emergency work, and therefore you can rest assured that your GSP is in very capable hands. However, this expertise often comes at a price, and after-hours consultations in specialist centers are usually considerably more costly than those at your local veterinary practice. In addition to this, these centers are not often open during the day, which means your dog will have to be transferred back to your local vet in the morning, then back again to the after-hours vet at night, which can be disruptive.

Extras

Another aspect to consider when choosing a veterinarian is whether they offer extra services other than veterinary consultations. This means you can take your dog to one place for all his needs. Other services might include a nutrition nurse, who can give specialist advice on food, a weight clinic, a dental clinic, puppy training and senior wellness checks. In addition to this, many veterinary practices also have a small store on-site, where you can buy food, toys, parasite control and accessories.

CHAPTER 12 Preventative Health Care

Vaccinations

Your first visit to the vet is likely to be when your puppy gets his first vaccination. This can be as young as six weeks old, depending on the brand of the vaccination. Some breeders may take your German Shorthaired Pointer puppy to get the first vaccination, so he will only need a booster four weeks later.

Vaccinations usually start with a course of two or three injections, followed by yearly boosters. They protect against some very serious canine diseases. If you are hesitant about vaccinating, the most important thing to do is at least take your puppy to have the initial course of two or three injections, and then test his immunity level yearly with a blood test. That way, you can just give a booster vaccination as and when the immunity levels drop.

The following are the diseases which are commonly vaccinated against:

- **Distemper** = This disease is a virus that can be devastating. It can cause non-specific symptoms, such as sneezing, vomiting, and coughing. It can also cause the hardening and thickening of the pads on the paws and of the nose. It rapidly progresses to death.
- **Parvovirus** = This is also a virus that typically affects young puppies. It causes bloody diarrhea, which is extremely contagious. This gradually causes puppies to fade due to dehydration and blood loss.
- **Leptospirosis** = Leptospirosis causes failure of the kidneys and liver, and the most common symptom is yellowing of the gums and eyes, known as jaundice. Some dogs also display neurological symptoms.
- **Hepatitis** = This is a virus, otherwise known as canine adenovirus, which like distemper causes some vague symptoms. Commonly seen are fatigue, fever, vomiting, diarrhea, and jaundice, and it will rapidly lead to death.
- **Parainfluenza** = This is sometimes contained in the injection which combines the four diseases already mentioned, or it can be part of the kennel cough vaccine. Parainfluenza is a virus, which can lead to a debilitating cough.
- **Kennel cough** = This is a vaccine that contains Bordetella and Parainfluenza. Together they create a complex disease known as kennel cough. It is highly contagious and causes a honking cough and a fever. This vaccine is squirted up the nose rather than injected.
- **Rabies** = This injection should be given as standard to any dog which lives in a rabies endemic area. It is a dangerous disease that causes

aggression, hypersalivation and neurological symptoms, which lead to death. If a rabid dog bites a human, the person also may contract the fatal disease.

Microchipping

In some parts of the world, such as the UK, microchipping is a legal requirement, but in the US, it simply comes as highly recommended. A microchip is a small metal implant which is inserted into the scruff of the neck via a needle. When scanned, a unique number is displayed on the scanner which correlates to your information on the microchip database. That way, you can be assured that if your GSP ever goes missing, he can be reunited with you with ease.

The microchip is smaller than a grain of rice, and the injection of it is very quick. It will cause your GSP a slight sting, which he will forget about a couple of minutes later.

Once inserted, the microchip provides a permanent link between you and your dog, as long as you remember to update your details with the microchip company if you move house or change cell phone number.

External Parasites

Depending on where you live geographically, different external parasites may be a threat to your dog. These include ticks, fleas, mites, lice and biting flies, such as sandflies.

External parasites can be picked up by your dog from other animals, and you can bring them into the house on your clothes also. Fleas, in particular, once established in your house, can be difficult to eradicate, as 95% of fleas live in the environment instead of on your dog. This means you have to treat both your dog and the environment for several months to make sure all fleas are killed as they hatch from their eggs. An easy test to see if your dog has fleas, is to rub the coat over a white kitchen paper towel, to remove some dirt and dust. When a small amount of water is dripped on the dirt, if it is flea dirt, it will stain the kitchen paper brown or dark red. However, they might be more obvious than that. Itchiness and seeing live fleas on your GSP will confirm there is an infestation.

Ticks on the other hand, don't usually cause discomfort, unless the bite becomes locally infected. The greater concern is that ticks can transmit dis-

CHAPTER 12   Preventative Health Care

eases to your dog, and therefore, should be removed quickly or prevented. It is worth keeping a tick hook on hand, which can be purchased from your vet, the pet store or online. A tick hook enables easy removal of the tick without touching it, and ensures the mouth parts are removed cleanly, as it is when these are left in the skin that infection can occur.

External parasite treatment can come in a variety of forms. Shampoos available from your local pet store are not always effective, and don't often have long lasting protection against parasites, so it is best to instead purchase prescription medication from your veterinarian. This ensures the drugs contained in them have minimal resistance and are safer for your dog. Prescription external parasite control can come in the form of spot-on pipettes, collars, pills and treats to suit your dog. They have different residual actions as well, with some lasting a month, and others offering up to eight months protection. Many external parasite treatments also come with the option of combining an internal parasite treatment too, to cover all parasitic needs.

Internal Parasites

Just as you should routinely treat for external parasites, you should also routinely treat for internal parasites. The most common types of worms include:

- **Intestinal roundworms and tapeworms:** These cause diarrhea, weight loss and bloating. In extreme cases, they can cause life-threatening gastrointestinal blockages.
- **Lungworms:** These worms stop blood from being able to clot, and can cause bleeding into the eyes. They also cause a cough, which can lead to respiratory distress since they cause damage to the lungs.
- **Heartworms:** These reproduce in the circulatory system, and can cause life-threatening blockages in the heart, arteries and small vessels in the lungs and leading to the brain.

Comprehensive worming treatments against roundworms and tapeworms are usually recommended every three months if your dog scavenges, or every six months if he doesn't. If you live in an area where lungworms are prevalent, it is actually best to deworm your dog with a roundworm treatment every month, and then with a tapeworm treatment every three months.

Neutering

If you don't plan to breed your German Shorthaired Pointer, which is not advisable if you are not a professional breeder, it is in his best interest to be neutered. In fact, you might be required to do this anyway, as some breeders require neutering in the sales contract, and rescue organizations almost always neuter their dogs.

If you are working your German Shorthaired Pointer, it is a common myth that an unneutered dog is a better working dog. In fact, it might be quite the opposite. A neutered male will not be so distracted by other dogs present in comparison to an entire male. And a neutered female won't have the issue of being in heat when required to work. Nevertheless, one thing that should be considered when neutering working dogs, or dogs which are likely to be active, is to wait until they are over a year old, and in the case of females, wait until three months after their first heat. The reason for this is that early neutering has been linked to cruciate ligament disease, which is discussed further in Chapter 13 as a condition to which German Short-

CHAPTER 12 Preventative Health Care

Photo Courtesy of Amanda Painter and Brad Duke

haired Pointers are at a higher risk. Therefore, delaying neutering by a few months may reduce your GSP's odds of suffering this condition.

Neutering males prevents unwanted matings, reduces the urge to roam which could lead to traffic accidents, prevents sexual frustration, reduces marking, reduces aggressive tendencies, reduces prostate conditions and eliminates cancers of the reproductive organs. Spaying a female will eliminate messy times when she is in heat, prevent unwanted pregnancies, reduce and almost eliminate the chances of mammary cancers, prevent uterine and ovarian cancers, and prevent a life-threatening uterine infection called a pyometra.

Both castration and spaying procedures require your dog to be a day patient at your local veterinary practice. He will need to be dropped off early on in the day, having had nothing for breakfast. The operation is usually done in the morning and your dog will usually be discharged in the afternoon, after a few hours of observation. The anesthetic will take the rest of the day to wear off, so don't worry if your GSP seems a little off color. You can give him some plain food, such as chicken and rice, and let him sleep for the rest of the day. By the next day, you should notice a big improvement.

In the two weeks following the operation, it is really important that you don't let your dog run around too much, jump up or lick at the incision. These exertions can cause the dog's stitches to come out and a wound infection to develop, which will significantly slow the healing and require extra medication. As a GSP puppy is naturally very exuberant, you may have to crate him during the healing period, and he may need to wear a buster collar or vest to prevent him from licking his stitches. Most vets like to check the incision after two to three days, and then again after 14 days to take out the stitches.

Pet Insurance

When first purchasing or adopting a German Shorthaired Pointer, one of the first things you should consider is taking out pet insurance. As discussed in Chapter 13, the GSP is prone to many genetic diseases which may be financially burdensome if you are not prepared for them. Some owners prefer to put away a sum of money each month to be prepared. Therefore, if not needed, you will have savings in the bank. Nevertheless, many pet owners find that pet insurance pays for itself and more, as well as giving peace of mind, and is a wise investment.

CHAPTER 12 Preventative Health Care

When deciding on which pet insurer to choose, you should read the fine print carefully. There are several different types of policies. Some give you a specific sum of money which you can use yearly for any condition, some will give you a smaller amount of money per year per condition, and some will have a maximum that can be spent on a condition for the lifetime of your dog. There's no right or wrong option, just find one will suit your pet best. For many insurance companies there are also three different levels of coverage, in addition to how the money is divided up:

- Accident coverage
- Accident and illness coverage
- Accident, illness and routine care coverage (which includes contributions towards vaccinations, parasite control, neutering, and dental care)

Older dogs may have a slightly different policy to younger dogs, as the insurance company takes on more risk if insuring an older dog for the first time. This might come in the form of a higher premium, or a higher excess which needs to be paid out when claiming for a condition.

Pet insurance will eliminate much of the worry of providing for your dog, as if something unexpected arises, you know that he will be covered. Therefore, by purchasing pet insurance, and providing the preventative veterinary measures which have been outlined in this chapter, you can ensure that you are giving your dog every opportunity to live a healthy, happy life.

CHAPTER 13
Breed-Specific Diseases

Photo Courtesy of Robert Esposito

One of the risks you take when purchasing a pedigree breed is that your dog might develop an inherited condition. The reason why these conditions are more common in pedigree breeds is because generally the gene pool is much smaller, resulting in a higher chance of faulty genes. Small gene pools can be due to line-breeding relatives, selective breeding when developing the breed, or simply due to fewer choices of matings compared to unlimited potential for crossbreeds.

The German Shorthaired Pointer is unfortunately not a particularly healthy breed when it comes to inherited conditions. However, it does not mean that if you get a GSP, he will definitely develop one or more of these conditions. And fortunately, some conditions can be tested for before two potential parents are bred. In addition to that, you can carefully question the ancestry of a puppy you're interested in, and establish whether any relatives developed conditions of concern which can't be tested for.

This chapter will look into some of the most common breed-specific diseases for German Shorthaired Pointers; however, it is not a fully inclusive list.

Diseases to Test For

As mentioned in Chapter 4, you should expect the following certification for both parents of a German Shorthaired Pointer:
- A recent certificate from the Canine Eye Registry Foundation (CERF). This includes an eye examination and a DNA test for progressive retinal atrophy.

CHAPTER 13   Breed-Specific Diseases

- A certificate from the Orthopedic Foundation of America (OFA) or PennHip certifying the dog to have normal hips. This is to test for hip dysplasia.
- A certificate from the Orthopedic Foundation of America (OFA) certifying the dog to have normal elbows. This is to test for elbow dysplasia.
- A recent certificate from the Orthopedic Foundation of America (OFA) or a report from a veterinary cardiologist certifying that the dog has had an Advanced Cardiac Examination and has a normal heart. This is to test for aortic stenosis.

Additionally, at least one parent should have a DNA test proving they are clear of a severe hereditary eye disease called Cone Degeneration (CD2), otherwise known as day blindness, as well as a bleeding disorder called von Willebrand's disease (VWDII). Only one parent is needed to test for these, as they are recessive genes, and therefore both parents must have the gene for a puppy to develop the condition.

The only thing that can be done to prevent these conditions is to be aware of them in the first place, and invest in a puppy with excellent pedigree where the parents have been tested. Here is more information about each of the conditions:

Progressive Retinal Atrophy

The retina is the back layer of the eye where the photoreceptor cells reside. The purpose of these cells is to convert light into a nerve signal for the brain to process as sight.

Photo Courtesy of Taylor Felger

When the retina atrophies, it means the cells deteriorate, leading to blindness. It often starts as night blindness and gradually progresses to total irreversible blindness. Luckily, GSPs are highly trainable dogs and adapt easily to their new normal, as long as you keep their surroundings the same.

Joint Dysplasia

Joint dysplasia can occur in the hips or the elbows, and is not immediately apparent. However, by the time your dog is fully grown, you can check whether your GSP has joint dysplasia with X-rays. Joint dysplasia is where the joints have skeletal abnormalities, and end up abnormally shaped.

This condition will worsen throughout a dog's lifetime, leading to joint degeneration and arthritis, which is likely to require chronic anti-inflamma-

Photo Courtesy of Megan Campbell

tory medication. Joint dysplasia, for a GSP in particular, is a terrible condition, as management involves controlled lead walks only, and no jumping or uncontrollable running for the entirety of a dog's life. A GSP with joint dysplasia will never be able to work in the field.

Aortic Stenosis

The aorta is a major vessel coming out of the heart, which transports blood to the rest of the body. Aortic stenosis is a condition where the exit of the heart into the aorta is narrowed, which can lead to turbulent blood, a murmur and weak pulses.

Aortic stenosis can sometimes be corrected by a surgical cardiologist, but milder cases can often be managed medically with heart medication. Mild cases can go on to live a relatively normal life, however it does increase the chances of secondary heart complications.

Cone Degeneration (Day Blindness)

In the retina in the eye, there are photoreceptors called 'cones' and 'rods.' Cones respond to bright light. Day blindness is a recessive genetic disease which causes the cones to degenerate, and difficulty seeing in bright light.

Day blindness develops between eight and 12 weeks of age and there is no cure.

Von Willebrand's Disease

Von Willebrand's disease is a genetic condition caused by a deficient concentration of von Willebrand factor (vWF) in the blood. vWF is essential to clot blood when there is a cut, and as a result, affected dogs may have bleeding from their gums, nose bleeds, blood in their urine, or bleed excessively after injections and wounds.

Von Willebrand's disease can be managed medically, and a blood transfusion prior to surgical procedures can minimize bleeding complications.

> **FUN FACT**
> **Best in Show**
>
> The 2016 winner of the Westminster Kennel Club annual dog show was a German Shorthaired Pointer named CJ, short for California Journey. CJ was the third GSP to win Best in Show, preceded by Traveler, who won in 1974, and Carlee, who won in 2005. Before winning Best In Show at the Westminster Kennel Club Show, CJ had already won 17 Best In Shows at only three years old.

Skin Diseases

The skin is one of the most important organs of the body. It is made up of three layers which protect all the internal organs. It also includes the hair, oil glands, sweat glands and claws, as well as muscles and fat underneath.

The skin is not only an important protective barrier against environmental threats, but it also helps to regulate temperature, and provides a sense of touch.

Photo Courtesy of Ginelle Woolcock

Skin health is highly correlated to an excellent diet and grooming care of your dog. A diet which is rich in omega-oils and essential vitamins will promote a strong skin barrier. It will also keep in line the commensal organisms on the skin, and promote a healthy production of natural waterproofing oils.

Genetic skin conditions are common, and most allergies also manifest as skin conditions. As a result, the skin often has more to contend with than environmental insults. For the GSP breed, lupus erythematosus, yeast dermatitis and acral mutilation syndrome are all genetically linked. Unfortunately, none of these can be tested for; however, when you obtain a puppy you can ask the breeder if they have any knowledge of previous generations which have suffered from these conditions.

Lupus Erythematosus

The most common type of lupus in the dog is 'systemic lupus erythematosus,' or SLE. However, the German Shorthaired Pointer is more prone to rarer forms, such as 'exfoliative cutaneous lupus erythematosus' (ECLE) and 'familial cutaneous lupus erythematosus' (CLE).

These conditions cause skin abnormalities, such as losing pigment in the skin, and the development of erosions and ulcers. They can also cause lethargy, lameness, and abnormalities within the blood. They first become apparent from a young age, typically under three years old.

Palliative medication can be given to manage the condition. Unfortunately, it is often not enough to ensure a good quality of life.

Yeast Dermatitis

Yeast dermatitis is a fungal skin condition caused by Malassezia pachydermatis. It is a normal commensal organism on the skin, but an overgrowth of it can cause the skin to flare up. It is known as an opportunistic pathogen, which means that it takes the opportunity to multiply when the skin is not in a good condition. The GSP in particular is genetically predisposed to yeast overgrowth.

A flare-up generally causes redness to the skin and itching. It might also cause crusty, flaky skin, and extend into the ears. It is usually accompanied by a characteristic musty odor.

It can be easily treated with medicated shampoos, however in severe cases, it might require several months of oral treatment.

Acral Mutilation Syndrome

Acral mutilation syndrome (AMS) is a rare genetic condition that alters the sensation of the extremities, such as the paws. The paws no longer feel temperature or pain.

It results in affected dogs obsessively licking their pads and paws, to the point where they are bleeding and ulcerated. This can then lead to bacterial and fungal infections which can be difficult to manage.

The condition requires anti-anxiety medication and an Elizabethan cone to prevent obsessive licking and self-trauma. It can be confirmed with genetic testing, but is not a test which is routinely performed prior to breeding.

Digestive Diseases

The digestive system comprises all the organs which are involved in digesting food. This not only includes the esophagus, stomach and intestines, which food passes through, but also the liver and pancreas, which are vital for producing bile and enzymes needed to break down the food into absorbable nutrients.

Digestive diseases can manifest in many different ways, from vomiting and diarrhea, to life-threatening blockages. Since nutrients from food are vital for any living being, problems with the digestive system can cause serious consequences.

Gastric Dilation Volvulus

Gastric dilation volvulus, or GDV, is a condition which German Shorthaired Pointers are prone to due to their deep chests. It occurs when the stomach becomes bloated with gas and twists around, leading to a blockage from the twist. It is a life-threatening condition and requires immediate medical attention. Common symptoms include a bloated appearance, collapse, unproductive retching, and severe abdominal pain.

In many cases, GDVs happen unexpectedly, however some precautions can be taken to minimize the risk of it happening. You should always feed your GSP a high-quality diet over two or three meals a day, rather than just one. And large meals and quick eating should be discouraged. Additionally, a dog should be exercised for an hour before and after meal-time.

Hepatitis

German Shorthaired Pointers, particularly females, are more likely to develop primary hepatitis than other breeds. This can be in response to toxins, drugs or infections.

Hepatitis is when the liver becomes inflamed and does not function appropriately. As a result, it doesn't filter out waste products effectively, which then build up in the system and cause your dog to feel sick and lethargic. The disease can also cause jaundice, which is a yellow color in the gums, eyes and skin, due to an increase of bilirubin in the blood.

The cause of the hepatitis needs to be confirmed to treat it effectively, which might require blood testing, ultrasound scans and a liver biopsy.

Myasthenia Gravis

Myasthenia gravis is a condition where the signal between the nerves and the muscles does not work. It results in extreme weakness and lethargy.

One of the main problems with myasthenia gravis is a condition called megaesophagus, which is when the esophagus which travels the food from the mouth to the stomach, dilates and holds food in it. As a result, afflicted dogs tend to vomit undigested food which has never reached the stomach. This can result in a higher risk of aspiration of the food, which can lead to pneumonia.

Myasthenia gravis can be medically managed, but some lifestyle changes are required. Raising the food and water bowls results in gravity aiding the food and water to pass down to the stomach, and small, frequent, high-quality meals are recommended. Exercise should also be limited, on account of the muscle weakness.

Mobility Diseases

Conditions which affect mobility usually target the musculoskeletal system. This system encompasses the bones, muscles, joints, tendons and ligaments. Any condition which affects mobility, affects the ability to exercise and work.

You can keep the musculoskeletal system healthy in a number of ways. Firstly, when your GSP is just a puppy, you should not over-exercise him. A minute for every week he is old is plenty. For example, if he is 15 weeks old, his walks should initially not be more than 15 minutes a day.

Photo Courtesy of Teri Buerkle

In addition to looking after the developing bones and joints, when your GSP is fully grown he should start a joint supplement. Joint supplements contain ingredients such as glucosamine, chondroitin and omega oils, which help lubricate the joint and improve cartilage health. This in turn improves the joint's ability to deal with concussive forces and gliding movements.

Finally, the best thing you can do for your GSP when it comes to preserving the musculoskeletal system, is to keep him lean and fit. In Chapter 8, body condition scoring and weight monitoring were discussed. You should try to keep your GSP at a score of five or just under, as this will prevent excess gravitational force on the whole body.

Cruciate Ligament Disease

The cranial cruciate ligament is a vital ligament in the stifle (knee) joint which is highly susceptible to injury. This can happen when your dog jumps or turns awkwardly, which for an active dog like the GSP is a frequent occurrence.

It is possible to reduce the risk of cruciate ligament injuries by neutering your dog a little later than usual, once he or she is fully grown. Many veterinary practices will routinely neuter between six and 12 months, but if the surgery is delayed until 18 months, the sudden change in hormones does not affect musculoskeletal development.

Cruciate ligament disease often requires surgery for the best outcome, as conservative management requires six to 12 weeks of crate rest (which is impossible for a bouncy GSP), and almost always leads to osteoarthritis further down the line.

Panosteitis

This is a painful condition where the outer surface of the long bones in the legs become inflamed. It is commonly likened to growing pains, as it happens in growing dogs between five and 14 months of age. Young male German Shorthaired Pointers are more at risk for developing panosteitis compared to females and other breeds.

The most common symptom is sudden, unexplained lameness, which may switch to one or more other legs and also resolve spontaneously after a few days to weeks. Even though it self-resolves, it requires pain relief, as some dogs become extremely sore when they have an episode.

***

German Shorthaired Pointers are prone to a wide range of diseases, many of which are genetic and relatively uncommon. By carefully selecting your puppy from tested parents, you will have the best chance to get a dog which will lead a healthy life. Nevertheless, all GSP owners should be aware of the potential diseases and be proactive in seeking veterinary advice if any of the symptoms become apparent.

CHAPTER 14
Adult Life

Your German Shorthaired Pointer is considered fully grown at 18 months, by which point his growth plates should have set. So finally, he is ready to burn off all that energy without risk of damaging his developing bones. However, the GSP is slower to mature mentally than the average dog, so during the first year that you take your GSP into the big outdoors, you will need to be especially careful to keep him safe.

You may have a job in mind for your adult GSP, such as guarding your home. Or you may wish to show off his good looks in dog shows or compete in sports and field trials. If his bloodlines are impeccable, you may even be thinking of breeding from your GSP. With such a versatile and multi-talented breed, there's a world of opportunity for you and your GSP as he reaches his adult years.

Photo Courtesy of Andrew Cannata

CHAPTER 14 Adult Life

Pet Life

As a pet, your GSP is definitely not destined for life as a couch potato! He was bred for endurance, and is brim-full of energy. Throughout his puppy years, you will have been teaching your dog obedience, and one of the most important lessons you will have taught him is solid recall, ready to enjoy all his adult years out and about in the countryside where he's most at home. You might also have been teaching your dog field training, as discussed in Chapter 7, as most hunting partners spend 98% of their time as pets, and only 2% of the time out in the field.

Photo Courtesy of Katelyn Cole

At this stage in your dog's development, there are a few important precautions to take, because your GSP is going to find his widening horizons very stimulating. He may temporarily lose sight of his training in the excitement. Plus, he is still mentally an adolescent and testing boundaries. So, the following supplies are indispensable during the first months that you take your dog out for strenuous outdoor exercise:

1. An ID tag on your dog's collar or harness, with the cell phone number of the phone that you actually have with you.
2. A harness to attach a leash to, so that any stresses are spread over the chest area and not the neck.
3. Ideally, a hands-free leash. These attach to a waist belt, and have an elasticated section, which works to keep your dog alongside you by dampening the contact without jolting him when he moves out of range.

In addition, you should also pack the following for your GSP:

1. A collapsible water bowl and flask, either in your backpack or the car
2. Poop bags to clean up after your dog
3. A first aid kit to clean any cuts or scrapes

4. A tick hook to remove any critters your dog might pick up
5. A towel to clean your GSP off before getting back in the car
6. A coat for your dog in cold or wet weather
7. Dog booties if you are tackling rugged terrain or snow

Running Partner

If you enjoy running to stay fit, your GSP will tackle any distance and any pace you care to throw at him with great enthusiasm! Do remember, though, that your GSP doesn't know his own limits. He will run through exhaustion and pain in the joy of the moment, and only pay for it later on. So, you should build up your runs with your dog by gradual increments, only pushing forward when you know your dog is comfortable with your existing distance and pace. This is new to him and he is building his fitness, even if you have been running for years.

When you plan to take your dog out on a run, do not feed him for at least two hours beforehand, or two hours afterwards, as GSPs are particularly susceptible to bloat. Also, the first few times you take your dog out, run in area you know well, where you know you won't meet traffic, cyclists, wildfowl, livestock, small animals, or a lot of other people.

It will take a few runs before your dog understands he is meant to be running by your side, and not bounding off in any direction he chooses.

Photo Courtesy of Claude Doucette

CHAPTER 14 Adult Life

Photo Courtesy of Christina Potter

The hands-free leash is very useful during this stage. Eventually, your dog should be reliable enough to run by your side off-leash. It can even be easier to keep your dog with you when you are running rather than walking, as he has speed, focus and direction to keep him on track and will be less distracted by his surroundings.

You should only run with your dog during the cooler parts of the day, as dogs can't regulate their temperature by sweating like we do, they can only pant to keep cool. So, they may easily suffer from heat stroke if exercised strenuously in hot temperatures.

Hiking Partner

If hiking is your thing, and you have access to long country trails, you will have no more willing a partner than the German Shorthaired Pointer! As with running, do observe your dog's limits, as he will keep going, fueled by adrenaline, but needs to build up his fitness and stamina. When hiking with your dog during the winter months or at high altitude, be aware that he is a shorthaired breed and susceptible to the cold. So, keep him out of icy water, consider a coat for him, and towel him off thoroughly when you're back at the car. If you're hiking in the snow, booties will stop the snow balling up between your dog's toes. Alternatively, petroleum jelly also helps prevent snow from packing in the paws.

If your hiking takes you through long grass, make sure you check your dog over for burrs and grass seeds as soon as you get home. Fortunately, with a shorthaired breed such as the GSP, your dog is less likely to bring home many souvenirs; however, certain grass seeds with barbs, such as foxtails, can lodge in the nose, ears and especially between the toes, where they may burrow into the skin and cause an infection, or even travel to other parts of the body.

If you've been hiking in an area where there are wild animals such as deer, your GSP may also pick up a tick. These may be hard to spot when you're at the car, because until they have fed, they are very small. However, once they have fed on your dog's blood, which may take a day or two, they enlarge to the size of a corn kernel. They commonly lodge around the ears, head, neck, groin, armpits and feet. If you feel a tick on your dog's skin, which is easy with a shorthaired breed, you shouldn't pull it off, as there is a danger of the mouth parts breaking off and staying embedded in your dog's skin. A tick hook allows you to gently lift the tick from the point of attachment, and twist it out with two or three rotations. Your dog should then be fine, but monitor the site for infection, or any signs of lethargy, lameness or lack of appetite in your dog that could indicate a tick-borne infection. These include Lyme disease, Ehrlichiosis, Anaplasmosis, Rocky Mountain Spotted Fever, Babesiosis, Bartonellosis, and Hepatozoonosis. Although these diseases are rare, if you are regularly hiking with your dog, a monthly spot-on treatment such as Frontline Plus or a Seresto collar is a good preventive measure.

Although rare, the most serious hazard to your dog when out hiking is being bitten by a venomous snake. In the USA these are the copperheads, cottonmouths (water moccasins), coral snakes and rattlesnakes (pit vipers). In the UK, the adder is the only venomous snake. As a dog owner, you should familiarize yourself with the appearance of the venomous snakes in

CHAPTER 14　Adult Life

your country. If you suspect your dog has been bitten by a venomous snake, you need to act quickly. Photograph the snake, if possible, for identification, and call the nearest vet. You then need to head straight to the veterinarian while exerting your dog as little as possible, as you do not want the venom to spread throughout his body. Loosen or remove his collar and harness in case of swelling that might restrict his airways, rinse or wipe the wound and if you have ice, apply it to the bite. Keep your dog as quiet and contained as possible in the car and turn up the AC to keep him cool. At the veterinary clinic, your dog will be treated with antivenom, which is sometimes specific to the snake that bit your dog, so this is where your photo ID will come in.

Copperhead Snake　　　　　　　　Coral Snake

Cottonmouth Snake　　　　　　　　Rattlesnake

Adder (Viper)

Fun Sport – Agility and Flyball

The German Shorthaired Pointer is one of the most fun-loving breeds out there with energy in abundance, so giving your dog a focus such as agility or flyball will not only exercise his body, but will give his brain a thorough work out as well. On top of this, it's enormous fun for both dog and owner!

FUN FACT
Ultimate Air Dog Champion

Seven, an athletic German Shorthaired Pointer, was named Ultimate Air Dog Champion at the Purina Incredible Dog Challenge when he jumped 30 feet and 4 inches into the air. The long-jump record is nearly a full 12 inches shorter than Seven's jump, at 29 feet, 4.5 inches, set by Mike Powell in 1991.

Agility and flyball are open to all dog breeds, and can be enjoyed just for fun, or as a competitive sport. If you wish to compete with your dog, you will need to join the Activity Register for the Kennel Club in your country. You don't need a pedigree certificate to compete in agility and flyball.

Agility and flyball should not be started until your dog is fully grown at 18 months, as these are high-impact sports that put stress on the musculoskeletal system, and to start while the growth plates are still soft could result in lasting disability or arthritis in later life.

Canine agility involves running with your dog around an obstacle course that comprises jumps, tunnels, weave poles, A-frames, elevated walkways and the see-saw. All this equipment is expensive, so the best way to get involved in agility is by joining your local club. Since it's also a competitive sport, it's best learned in company, and with the instruction of an expert. However, if you live in a remote area but would still like to have fun teaching your dog agility, you can find excellent tutorials online, and can make improvised jumps and obstacles. Be aware that your jumps should be very low when your dog starts learning, and must only be raised as his body and skills develop. In an agility club, this will be determined by measuring your dog, and expert evaluation of his fitness and ability.

Flyball consists of a straight course of several jumps, with a box at the end that releases a ball when the dog makes contact with it. The activity takes the form of a relay race, where each dog is sent out on his own over the jumps to retrieve the ball, and return the same way. As a team activity, it isn't really a sport suited to the back yard, you need to find a club to enjoy flyball. You can however practice the skills your dog needs for flyball at home. These are catching, fetching and bringing back a ball, and being able to send your dog out over jumps on his own.

All the obedience training and bonding you have done with your dog during his first 18 months will have set the perfect foundation for the focus and attention your dog needs for agility and flyball. And giving him a fun job to do will help him take those skills to the next level!

CHAPTER 14 Adult Life

Guard Dog Life

The people-loving German Shorthaired Pointer is not the first breed most people would think of when it comes to a guard dog. However, when the breed was first developed in 19th-century Germany, the GSP would have been brought back to the family home at the end of the day's hunting, to alert against intruders during the night.

For most owners, barking is an undesirable behavior. But if you live in an area where you need security, a dog that can be extremely vocal about

Photo Courtesy of Abigail DeLay

the presence of strangers on his territory is a positive attribute. Your GSP is unlikely to physically attack an intruder, which can save you all sorts of legal problems, but he will certainly let you know if there is someone on your property. In most cases, a barking dog is enough for an intruder to leave empty-handed.

If you want your GSP to be a guard dog, it's highly recommended that you find a professional trainer. This is to make sure your dog differentiates between friends and strangers. But it is important to work alongside your trainer in teaching your dog his job. Maintaining obedience and respect is vital for a guard dog. This is because you are encouraging him to be reactive, which can backfire if discipline isn't maintained.

Photo Courtesy of Zachary Lewis

Your dog needs to know the boundaries of his territory, so you should regularly take him around the perimeter of your property. Teach him educated barking, by involving people that you know but which your dog doesn't. Ask them to approach your property, and encourage your dog to bark. Reward him for this behavior. But you also need to teach your dog when to stop barking, by withholding the reward until he is quiet, then using the "Quiet" command and treating him.

(If you are not training a guard dog, but you have a problem barker, the same technique applies. Don't shout at your dog for barking, as to his ears, you are joining in the chorus. Instead, wait for a break in the noise, say "Quiet," and reward him for his silence.)

Whereas it's common for traditional guard dog breeds to live out in the yard 24/7, the GSP isn't ideally suited to living outdoors overnight or in cold weather. This is due to his thin coat, and also his need to be with his humans. If you wish your GSP to be a guard dog, his attentive hearing can alert you to the presence of strangers from his place inside the house.

Show Life

As a pedigree breed with stunning good looks, you may wish to enter your German Shorthaired Pointer in dog shows. There are two main types of showing available to you as the owner of a GSP. The shows that immediately spring to mind are the conformation classes, where your dog will be judged on how closely he conforms in his physique and temperament to the breed standard. The breed standard varies between countries, and it can occasionally be updated, so you should look it up on your country's Kennel Club website. The American Kennel Club's breed standard for the GSP may be found in Chapter 2.

It's important to note that the AKC currently requires the GSP to be docked, although docking has been condemned by the American Veterinary Medical Association. Although the AKC does not disqualify an undocked dog, your GSP may be penalized in the show ring, so you need to be aware of this when selecting your puppy. However, in countries such as the UK where docking is illegal, only undocked GSPs may be shown in conformation classes. The breed standard does, however, acknowledge docking, since as a working dog, the GSP is permitted to be docked if it can be evidenced the dog is intended to work. This has to be carried out by a vet before the puppy is 5 days old, and a legally docked dog must be certified and microchipped. In the UK, docked GSPs may only enter working classes such as field trials and competitions on the Activity Register.

In most countries, to compete in Kennel Club conformation classes, a dog must be unneutered. This is because shows are more than just beauty pageants, they exist to promote the very best bloodlines for breeding. In the UK it is possible to obtain a "permission to show letter" for a neutered dog to compete. However, in practice, the dog will be at a disadvantage when the ribbons are handed out.

Also, in order to compete in Kennel Club shows, your dog will need to be registered on the Breed Register. Your breeder may have already done this when you collected your puppy with all his paperwork. If not, this can be done on the Kennel Club website. This is also an excellent place to find shows that your dog can enter. Although puppy classes are often available, most classes require your dog to be over 6 months of age.

If you are new to showing, it's well worth attending as many dog shows as possible before entering your dog. This is to familiarize yourself with what is expected, and if you bring your dog along, it will accustom him to all the noises and distractions. You can also find videos of dog shows online, to help you pick up tips and techniques. It's also worth entering your dog in local companion shows in a relaxed environment, before ramping up the pressure in higher level competitions. If your GSP isn't Kennel Club registered, he can still enter most local fun dog shows.

Joining your country's breed club will also open up showing opportunities, as well as providing support, and the camaraderie of being part of a group of fellow GSP enthusiasts.

The second type of showing competitions draws upon your GSP's talents and versatility. These are activity competitions such as field trials, coursing, tracking and obedience. Your dog doesn't necessarily need to belong to the Breed Register to compete in most activities, although you will have to join the Activity Register or Canine Partners. This opens up higher level competition for those whose GSP came without papers, perhaps through rescue, or those who have a GSP-crossbreed. If you work your GSP in the field, he might be particularly good at these types of shows, but it is important to note a GSP for Kennel Club showing shows and a GSP for field work are quite different. Therefore, if you want to show your GSP, aim to buy your dog from a breeder who breeds show dogs, and likewise, if you want to work your GSP, aim to buy your dog from a breeder who works their dogs.

CHAPTER 14   Adult Life

Stud Life

There are many reasons why people choose to breed from their GSP. Firstly, the breed is beautiful, and what could be more satisfying than propagating those magnificent genes? Secondly, puppies are cute, and it's a common perception that it will be fun to breed a litter. Thirdly, plenty of people believe it is only right that any dog should experience parenthood. Fourthly, it would be educational for the children! And fifthly, breeding pedigree dogs is an easy way to make a quick buck.

All of these are very bad reasons to breed from your German Shorthaired Pointer!

It's highly recommended that all breeding be left to the professionals, and especially with a pedigree breed, the integrity of the breed can only be upheld in the most responsible breeding environment, fully regulated by the Kennel Club, and with all the experience and investment of those who are fully committed to producing the healthiest ambassadors for the breed. The finest dogs are produced from the very best genetics, carefully maintained and refined over generations.

Dog breeders fall into two categories, professional breeders and hobby breeders. If you are considering becoming a hobby breeder, there are a few things you need to consider before mating your dog.

Whether you have a male or a female German Shorthaired Pointer, your dog needs to be registered with the Kennel Club in your country, and so does the dog you intend to mate yours with. This is to ensure that the puppies can also be Kennel Club registered. You are also obliged to have your dog fully health tested for the conditions mentioned in Chapter 4. These are hip and elbow scores, an eye examination, heart check, and DNA tests for the conditions common to the German Shorthaired Pointer. These tests are expensive but necessary, or the litter may endure a lifetime of suffering.

Mating takes place in one of three ways. A natural mating, or live breeding, occurs when the animals are allowed to meet and mate as nature intended. This should not be allowed to happen without careful supervision, as occasionally the male will be injured if the female breaks away while he is tied in position. To avoid injury, sometimes the male and female are mated artificially side-by-side. Or artificial insemination may be carried out with shipped-in semen, and the two dogs may never meet. If you own the female, you will need to pay a stud fee that will vary according to your method and the quality of the male. If you travel your female to the male, you will have travel and accommodation costs. If you own the male, you will ei-

Photo Courtesy of Rodney and Robin Haddock

ther have to be comfortable with the risk of injury to your dog, or with producing and handling semen from your dog, and the process of inseminating the female.

With a litter of puppies comes great responsibility. You have the responsibility to face that not all the pups may be born equally healthy, and some may have to be euthanized, or you will have medical costs in trying to save them. Pups create a lot of mess, so your hygiene needs to be meticulous for the health of mom and her puppies. It's your responsibility to play with the pups throughout their first 2-3 months with you, so they are well socialized when they go to their new homes. Finally, puppies need suitable housing, food, vet checks and shots during their time with you. Because of all these expenses, good breeders don't get rich, so profit should never be your motivation for breeding from your GSP.

CHAPTER 14 Adult Life

If you are in the US, you will have to make a hard decision about docking your litter of pups. If your potential customers have ambitions to show their dogs, or if they intend to work them, they will be looking for a docked dog. On the other hand, docking has been condemned by the American Veterinary Medical Association, and many people consider it inhumane. In the UK and other countries where docking is illegal, you don't have this dilemma, unless your dogs are destined for a working life, in which case they are exempted. However, as this would need to be evidenced to a vet before the puppies are 5 days old, your buyer would need to be involved from birth.

Finally, if you are the owner of the female GSP involved in the mating, and you have raised the pups, fed them, nurtured them, played with them and recognized all their individual character traits over the 2-3 months they have spent with you, the time will come when you have to send them off to their new homes. This is the time of ultimate responsibility, and as a breeder, you are entirely within your rights to question each potential owner carefully to ensure your precious pups are going to continue receiving the best possible care. You also have a moral obligation to take back any dog if the home doesn't work out, so you need to consider the practical implications of this.

If, having accepted all the conditions of breeding responsibly, you decide to breed a litter from your GSP female, or use your male dog to mate with another GSP, you should do your homework thoroughly, and always keep the end goal in sight; the production of robustly healthy dogs from fully screened parents of impeccable temperaments. That way, you will protect the integrity and the reputation of the German Shorthaired Pointer.

***

Your German Shorthaired Pointer can be destined for a number of directions in his adult life, and his boundless energy and trainability can allow him to become so much more than a sedentary pet. But whatever job you choose for your GSP, as long as it is rooted in a strong relationship with you and diligent training, your GSP is sure to make you proud.

CHAPTER 15
Living with a Senior Dog

Getting old is an inevitable part of life, and unfortunately, dogs simply don't seem to live long enough. If your German Shorthaired Pointed has reached his double figures, you will probably start to notice him slowing down in several ways. A dog is considered senior over the age of eight years old. An older dog is prone to more issues than younger dogs; however, the good news is that if you are aware of this and make appropriate changes, you can have many more healthy years with him.

Photo Courtesy of Ryan Johnson

Diet

All senior dogs should be fed a senior diet. This is quite different from an adult dog diet and will benefit your aging dog greatly. The main aspect of a senior dog diet is that it contains fewer calories. This is because older dogs tend to be more sedentary in their later years, even if your GSP has been a livewire for most of his life. His activity levels are likely to decrease as he ages, and if you had a hunting dog, in his old age he's probably retired or only going on shorter hunts. Therefore, fewer calories are needed. If he's fed a higher number of calories, this can put your GSP at risk of putting on weight, which can stress the joints and vital organs such as the heart and kidneys.

Senior dog diets usually contain higher levels of omega-3 and omega-6. These essential fatty acids are excellent at improving the health of aging joints, by improving the lubrication of the joint as well as having natural anti-inflammatory properties. They also improve the health of the eyes, heart and brain, all of which may deteriorate with age.

Diets for senior dogs also often have supplements in them, such as glucosamine, chondroitin and probiotics. If they don't, you can add these to your dog's diet separately, as they also help improve the health of senior dogs. Glucosamine and chondroitin are considered the most scientifically effective supplements for improving joint health, by providing the building blocks of joint cartilage. This ensures the joints can move smoothly and comfortably. Probiotics are also helpful for senior dogs and can aid your dog's digestive system, which often becomes more sensitive with age. Probiotics are healthy bacteria that line the gut and help your dog to digest food. They also compete with bad bacteria and play a function in improving the immune system.

If you decide to switch your older GSP to senior food, this doesn't have to be done as soon as he turns eight years old. Nor does it have to be done quickly. The best way to alter a diet is to discuss matters with your vet and then slowly introduce the new food, more and more each day, over about a week. This allows you to phase in the new diet and phase out the old while looking for any reactions from your GSP.

CELEBRITY DOGS

Samson Cooper

Bradley Cooper, an American actor and filmmaker, rescued his German Shorthaired Pointer, named Samson, from a kill shelter three weeks before the dog was scheduled to be euthanized. When Samson passed away at the ripe age of 15 in 2011, Cooper had a giant photograph of his beloved companion installed in his home. "They're my kids," Cooper once said when speaking about his dogs.

Photo Courtesy of Amy Lobato

CHAPTER 15   Living with a Senior Dog

Senior Wellness Checks

Your vet is there to help you with your dog and should play an important role in keeping your elderly GSP healthy. Preventative healthcare is paramount to ensure your dog has a long and happy life. Detecting ailments early and treating them before they've had the chance to develop will ensure the best outcome for your GSP.

Senior wellness checks should be carried out at least once yearly from when your dog is eight years old. If your dog has complicated ailments or is on chronic medication, twice yearly is better. A senior health check can be carried out at the same time as an annual vaccination to prevent too many stressful visits to the vet.

Your vet will start the checkup by weighing your dog. Keeping your GSP lean puts less strain on his joints and heart, and will keep him active for longer. Therefore, if he has started to increase in weight, your vet might want to talk to you about changing his diet.

Next, the vet is likely to perform a clinical examination. He will pay particular attention to your dog's teeth, eyes, heart and lungs, all of which can degenerate with age. He is also likely to feel your GSP's abdomen to make sure there are no masses, as cancers are more common with age, and then the vet will check your dog's skin and coat to ensure they are in good health.

After the physical examination, a blood test will be done to assess the underlying health of your GSP's organs, which take on more strain as your dog gets older. The organs of concern are mainly the kidneys and the liver, although the blood test will analyze your dog's health as a whole. Your vet might also do a blood pressure measurement, which will indicate whether there are any heart or kidney problems.

Advanced Arthritis

Osteoarthritis, also known as arthritis, is a degenerative condition that affects all the structures of the joint. Most dogs in their older age are affected by arthritis, which is painful to a varying degree. Arthritis is triggered due to several reasons:

- The joint is abnormal, for example, has had an injury in the past or has joint dysplasia, and normal gravitational forces are exerted on it.
- The joint is normal, but abnormal gravitational forces are exerted on it, for example, due to excess weight.

- The joint has been subjected to extensive wear and tear, for example, the high activity of a working or athletic dog.

Within the joint, the joint fluid, joint cartilage, subchondral bone (bone underneath the cartilage) and the joint lining all degenerate, which leads to a joint that does not glide smoothly and cannot withstand concussive forces.

The best way to manage arthritis is with multimodal management. That means multiple forms of treatment. If your GSP doesn't have any underlying health conditions, your veterinarian can prescribe anti-inflammatories to help the joints. In addition to this, if your GSP is carrying extra weight, this should immediately be addressed by putting him on a diet. Joint supplements can also aid in improving the joint, which include omega oils (to improve joint fluid viscosity and volume, as well as provide natural anti-inflammatory effects) and glucosamine or chondroitin (to improve cartilage and joint fluid composition).

You might also want to consider complementary therapies to help your dog stay active. Veterinary physiotherapists can give you exercises to do at home, to keep your dog stretched and supple, as well as offer hydrotherapy which is a great way for your dog to stay fit without extra strain being put on the joints. Specialist trained veterinarians can also perform acupuncture, which is an excellent pain reliever without the need for drugs.

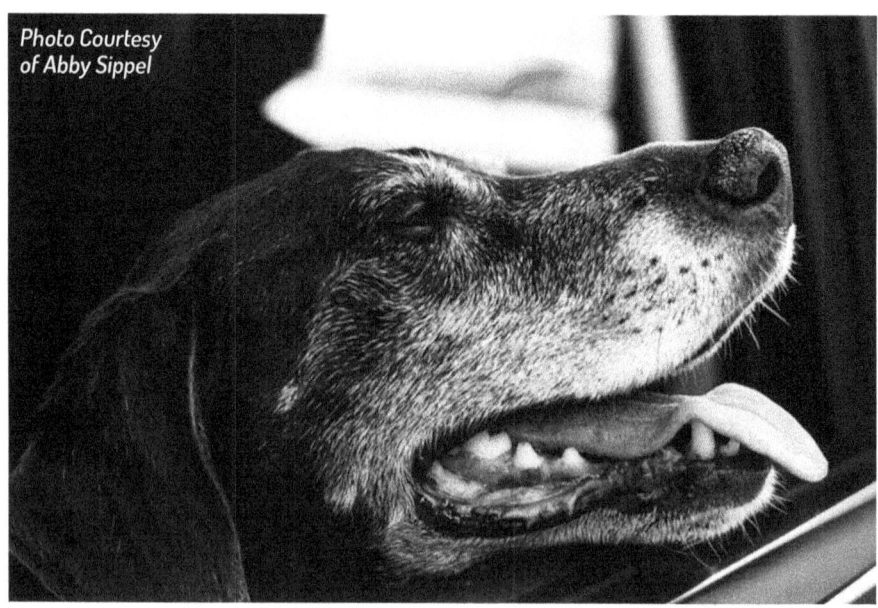

Photo Courtesy of Abby Sippel

CHAPTER 15 Living with a Senior Dog

Photo Courtesy of Jan and Stephen Roberts

Mental Deterioration

Until fairly recently, it was widely accepted that dogs lost some cognitive function as they aged; however, there is now a recognized condition called Canine Cognitive Dysfunction. This is very similar to dementia in humans. So, if you find your elderly GSP is not the dog he used to be, there is a strong possibility that this is what he is suffering from.

The most common symptoms of CCD are dullness, lethargy, aimless wandering, urinating or defecating in abnormal areas when previously housebroken, and waking up at unusual times in the night.

Even though there is no cure for CCD, there is excellent medication available from your veterinarian. This medication improves the blood flow to the brain, which enables it to receive more oxygen and function better. You may find that this medication will give your old GSP a whole new lease of life.

Organ Deterioration

During the lifetime of any dog, the kidneys and liver are two organs which work extremely hard to filter waste products from the body. As a result, they can start to deteriorate in your GSP's senior years.

Symptoms may include loss of appetite, vomiting, drinking more, and urinating more. In addition to this, liver disease may cause jaundice, which presents as yellow gums, and kidney disease may cause anemia, which presents as pale gums. Your veterinarian will assess the health of your dog's internal organs through a blood test, and if he is concerned, may carry out an ultrasound examination. Your GSP might not be experiencing any of these symptoms however, which is why senior wellness checks are so important. Both the kidney and liver can function with as little as 20% capacity, so problems can go a long time unnoticed. Picking up on early degeneration will ensure that your dog has the best chance of a good prognosis.

There are excellent diets available for management of kidney disease and liver disease in older dogs, which is the main method of treatment. These diets reduce pressure on the liver and kidneys. In addition to that, there are medications available to help improve the efficiency of the organs, which a veterinarian will be able to dispense.

Sometimes, in older dogs, the heart also deteriorates. This is usually due to valves inside the heart becoming leaky. This can lead to some backflow and congestion. Symptoms include listlessness, fainting, coughing, and getting out of breath easily. Starting heart medication early will reduce the pressure on the heart and significantly increase your dog's life span.

Alongside the heart lie the lungs. Usually, the lung tissue is fairly elastic, which allows it to expand and contract as air is breathed in and out. An older dog's lungs become more fibrous with age; they don't expand as well. This might lead to an inability to fight off infections.

While it might sound like an elderly dog is always in poor health, picking up on changes early, and making alterations to your GSP's lifestyle will ensure that your dog stays as healthy as possible.

CHAPTER 15 Living with a Senior Dog

Loss of Senses

It is common for elderly dogs to lose some of their senses, particularly sight and hearing. When one sense goes, often the others are fortified through compensating, and deaf or blind dogs can live happy, long and highly functional lives.

Photo Courtesy of Dawn and Tim Van De Mark

GSPs are highly intelligent dogs and teaching your dog coping mechanisms will help him adjust to his new world. Teaching commands such as 'slowly,' 'wait,' 'turn' and 'stop' will prevent him from getting into trouble if he starts losing his sight. He will also be able to navigate his way around the house with ease, as long as you keep the furniture in the same place, as his memory of navigating spatial areas will still be excellent.

When a dog loses his hearing, this is slightly more difficult to manage. It is a good idea to preempt hearing loss at some point in your dog's life. To do this, when you teach him commands as a puppy, always combine a voice command with a signal. That way, if your dog loses some or all of his hearing, he will still be able to understand you. Hearing loss is usually gradual though, and it is likely that you will not realize he is losing his hearing until it is quite far advanced. You might even initially think it is the stubbornness of the GSP breed causing him to ignore you.

Bladder Control

At the exit of the bladder is a muscular band called the urethral sphincter. It stops the urine from free-flowing out of the bladder, until your dog decides it's time to potty. Unfortunately, in elderly dogs, this sphincter is not always entirely effective and occasionally urine can leak. This is not the fault of your dog and you should not punish him for urinating in the house by accident.

For female dogs, the most common reason for the sphincter to become leaky is a condition called urinary sphincter mechanism incompetence (USMI). This happens because the muscular sphincter has more tone in it if your dog has had estrogen in her system for some of her life. If she is spayed before her first season, she will never have had reproductive hormones in her blood stream and the necessary estrogen to tighten up the sphincter. As a result, later in life, it does not always hold in the urine. This is easily treated by supplementing with estrogen, which is a daily tablet that significantly improves the leakage.

For male dogs, and sometimes also females, the main reason for leakage is a problem with the nerves. The nerves originate in the lower spine, and if there are problems in this area, the sphincter does not receive all the neurological signals necessary for it to stay shut. The most common problem in the lower spine is a degenerative process call spondylosis, which like arthritis results in bony growth which can compress on the spinal cord. Medications can improve the symptoms; unfortunately,

CHAPTER 15   Living with a Senior Dog

Photo Courtesy of Peter Sempie

however, the primary cause cannot be treated, and may require intensive treatment, as spinal conditions can be painful and affect the quality of life of your dog.

Lifestyle Modifications

Having a senior dog will soon make you realize that some things will need to be modified in your house, especially when your dog reaches his final senior years. An older dog, especially one with joint issues, is not as mobile as he was in his younger years, and may struggle to jump and play as he did before. If you have allowed your GSP on the furniture when he was younger, you cannot stop him from doing it in his later years, even though it is better for his joints to avoid the jarring forces from jumping on and off. You might want to consider buying steps or a ramp to place by your sofa or bed, as well as a ramp for your car, as a GSP is too heavy to always lift up and down yourself.

In addition, he will need to play more gentle games. Tug of war is not a good idea, as it can put excess strain on his fragile spine and joints. Fetch is still fine as long as your dog does not get overly enthusiastic. Scenting games, regardless of whether your dog has worked in his lifetime or not, are also great to play with an older dog as it helps keep his mind sharp and doesn't put physical strain on his aging body.

Saying Goodbye

When it comes to the final days of your dog's life, it can be a very emotional time. Sometimes it is clear cut, and other times it may not be so obvious when you should make the decision. But regardless of the situation, your vet will be able to advise you about the health of your dog and whether their quality of life is compromised. When it comes to quality of life, there are three questions you should consider: Does your GSP still want to eat? Does he still wag his tail and seem happy at times? And does he still interact with you? If his condition causes you to answer no to those questions, and nothing more can be done to improve his well-being, then it might be time to consider putting him to sleep.

The injection will be done by your veterinarian, and while it is a sad time, it is usually a very peaceful procedure. Your veterinarian may start by sedating your GSP, and then placing a catheter in the vein in his leg. Once you've said your goodbyes, an overdose of anesthetic is given. This is non-painful and causes the brain to go into a deep sleep before stopping the heart. It only takes a matter of seconds. Your vet will then check the heart to confirm he has passed away. The injection can be given at home, at the vet practice, or in your car. The important thing is that it is done somewhere that your dog will feel calm.

Saying goodbye is always hard, but in the end, it is an act of love that you can peacefully end his suffering. While you are bound to feel sad about the loss of your companion, you should try to find comfort in remembering all the wonderful times that you have had with your GSP, and how much joy he has brought you over the years.

www.ingramcontent.com/pod-product-compliance
Lightning Source LLC
Chambersburg PA
CBHW060044230426
43661CB00004B/650